"I've had the pleasure of watching Nick grow into a man. His father, Paul, and I were on the staff at Oklahoma State in 1992. Nick has always had a passion for hoops and a very caring heart for others, which is apparent in his book. He takes biblical principles and presents them in a way that today's athletes and coaches can identify with and relate to, which is why *God x Basketball* is a must-read. I found it uplifting and motivating, and I look forward to having my Kansas University players read it and become better for it."

—**Bill Self,**
Kansas University Head Coach,
Basketball Hall of Famer

"Because of Nick's life experiences, I believe this book will have a greater reach than expected. Regardless of our position in sports, a meaningful and consistent walk with Christ will allow all of us to grow in a way that matters for eternity. This book will aid in that development."

—**Buzz Williams,**
Texas A&M Head Basketball Coach

"I've had the pleasure of getting to know Nick better over the last few years. I'm not surprised at his ability to develop players on the court. He's a coach's kid who played at a high level. What's been both surprising and most impressive about Nick is his passion for developing athletes off the court. With his book, *God x Basketball*, Nick leverages his enthusiasm and experiences in basketball to relate to and connect with athletes and coaches alike to strengthen their faith. Well done!"

—**Frank Haith,**
University of Tulsa Head Basketball Coach

"*God x Basketball* delivers a great message of how to apply God's written Word to the life of any athlete. It's easy to understand and apply to daily life. Well done."

—**Jimmy Dykes,**
ESPN College Basketball Analyst

"When I met Nick, I was coming off the hardest season I've ever had. I was broken mentally and physically, but most off all spiritually. Nick instantly became more than just an exceptional trainer to me. He became a genuine friend. Nick encouraged me through the Word of God. Not only did my game elevate, but my relationship with God grew, which led to my return to the NBA and leading my team to a championship while playing overseas. This book motivates you through God's Word to be all you can be on and off the court."

—**Julyan Stone,**
NBA Professional Basketball Player

"Nick and his book *God x Basketball* helped provide a lot of clarity and wisdom during my college career and in life. He gives advice that's authentic, relatable and, most importantly, the truth!"

—**Kareem South,**
Professional Basketball Player

"I met Nick during my time with the Denver Nuggets. What pleases me most about Nick, a man of faith, is not his on-court coaching but the impact he's had on athletes outside the lines. Nick has allowed God to work through him to create a culture that continues to produce character in athletes. Nick's basketball-themed devotionals encourage me in my journey as a coach for Christ, and *God x Basketball* will do the same for its readers."

—**Melvin Hunt,**
Assistant Coach, Atlanta Hawks, NBA

"Nick was huge in developing who I am today, both on and off the basketball court. From the time I was a youngster, he challenged me to strive toward excellence in whatever I was doing. He also influenced me never to compromise my character. His book, *God x Basketball*, will do the same for developing players. I can confidently say I wouldn't be a college basketball player today if it weren't for Nick's guidance."

—**Sam Masten,**
Men's Basketball Player, University of Northern Colorado

"Meeting Nick was a blessing and a great thing for me. I didn't really know much about God or the Bible. After spending time with Nick at a Christian leadership camp for basketball players, I felt closer to God than I had ever been. I read my first Bible scripture with Nick. During my rookie year as a professional, I called Nick because I was struggling, and his words of encouragement helped me tremendously. Nick is a great mentor and friend to have in your corner. Through his book, *God x Basketball*, I am certain that he will have the same impact on its readers that he has had on me over the years."

—**Marcus Stroman,**
Professional Basketball Player

"Nick is not just a friend; he is also an extremely positive influence on my life. He has mentored countless kids who have gone on to be successful not only in athletics but also in other fields and professions. He is passionate, hardworking, and practices what he preaches. He has helped me make leaps and bounds in my career by assisting me in developing into a better player and person. I appreciate him as a friend, and this book is something that every young basketball player and athlete should read to reach their full potential."

—**Jimmer Fredette,**
2011 National College Player of the Year,
NBA Professional Basketball Player

"Author Nick Graham takes us on a spiritual journey using sports as the vehicle. *God x Basketball* will help you realize that we are not human beings having a spiritual experience but rather spiritual beings having a human experience. When life throws you an 'adversity assist,' your faith must be strong enough to finish the play. *God x Basketball* is the playbook designed to help your faith lead you through any adversity life throws your way."

—**Sundance Wicks,**
Assistant Basketball Coach, University of Wyoming

"Nick became more than a mentor to me. He is someone I can come to no matter what, basketball or personal life. His guidance helped me develop as a basketball player and as a person while keeping God in the center. *God x Basketball* will not only be relatable for players but will also motivate players to be their very best at all times."

—**Adrianna Camber,**
Iowa State Women's Basketball

"When you mix honesty and integrity with direction and dedication, you get Nick Graham. Nick began training our son, Braeden, when he was 10. Nick has been an integral part of Braeden's development as an athlete and his walk with Christ. Nick's knowledge of the game along with his discipleship provides an abundance of worth for athletes. Nick's book proves to be a powerful tool. There is strength between his lessons and scripture that can change a life. We are so excited for his book and all the many more lives he's about to touch."

—**Gerard and Heather Byrne,**
Parents of Braeden Byrne, Competitive Youth Athlete

"Nick began working with my son Colin during his ninth-grade year. We assumed Nick was just a basketball trainer who could help Colin develop his skills. It did not take long to realize that Nick was much more than that. Within a few sessions, Nick tapped into Colin's mental and held him to a standard of excellence. What makes Nick different are the mentorship, faith, and inspiration he provides. The way Nick incorporates scripture and basketball not only helps my son push through adversities but also helps me. Nick has been able to capture that in this book."

—**Lee Smith,**
Father of Colin Smith, Competitive Youth Athlete

"I met Nick during my fourth year of college, and immediately I knew he was someone I wanted to be around. He helped me grow my game by working with me on the court, and he also made a great effort to make sure I was getting fed spiritually by leading a group Bible study at our basketball facility. The same energy that he put into investing in me and the other athletes around me, he put in this book. I know readers can gain so much valuable insight and knowledge by picking up this book and reading it."

—**Alexa Middleton,**
Iowa State Women's and Professional Basketball Player

"Nick never lets me settle for less than God's best. When I was younger, I didn't understand. Now, at 22 years old, I realize those experiences have aided me in overcoming all adversity that has stood between me and my dream of being a major college basketball player. Being around Nick has caused me to elevate my game in basketball, my personal life, and my relationship with God. His book, *God x Basketball*, relates to athletes by using athletic experiences to better understand God's Word, and I'm confident that all who read it will elevate their games as well."

—**Jervae Robinson,**
Washington State University Basketball

"I have known Nick since I was a freshman in high school. Nick helped my teammates and me at Dallas Skyline improve on the court, which led to us not only being one of the best teams in Texas but also the nation. His off-court impact was most beneficial, and he contributed to our character development as young men. I'm excited for my fellow athletes to read his book, *God x Basketball*, to be able to win in life and basketball. This is a one-of-a-kind book. Nick's ability to use hoops and relate it to everyday life makes it easy to read and understand."

—**Marcus Garrett,**
University of Kansas Basketball,
2020 Naismith Defensive Player of the Year

"Nick is one of a kind. His ability to reach people, challenge people, and motivate others while also showing the ability to lead and show compassion is what makes Nick special. What makes Nick most special is his love for the Lord and his ability to be open about his faith. I know for a fact that Nick is going to change a lot of lives with *God x Basketball*."

—**Trey Moses,**
Ball State, Professional Basketball Player

"Nick Graham is a servant leader and life coach who seeks out ways to be a light and make a positive impact in people's lives. His faithfulness, dedication, and selflessness have shaped my perspective over the years, and this book will do the same."

—**Brad Davison,**
University of Wisconsin Men's Basketball

"I had the opportunity to get to know Nick Graham during my time on staff at the University of Denver. Nick is one of the most genuine people I know. He has an extreme passion for basketball and helping people. Both of these passions are very apparent in his book. *God x Basketball* is a must-read that both today's coaches and athletes can relate to. I look forward to utilizing it with my fellow coaches and athletes at Belmont Abbey College and each school I have the opportunity to coach at."

—**Zach Ruebesam,**
Assistant Basketball Coach, Belmont Abbey College

"In my over two decades-long friendship with Nick, I've seen him grow from a curious young hooper to a grown young man who knows his two passions, God and basketball. He and I have spent countless hours discussing how we can impact and influence the next generation. I'm extremely proud of the man Nick has become, and his book, *God x Basketball*, will make a significant impact on all who read it. I will sit back and continue to enjoy his growth and impact."

—**Chauncey Billups,**
NBA Champion, NBA Finals MVP

"I've had the pleasure of competing against Nick during his playing days at Washington State. It's incredibly refreshing to see him apply his experience in hoops to his faith and use that recipe as a vehicle to encourage others. This book is a gem and is the perfect playbook to assist its readers not only on their journey through sports but life as well."

—**Mark Few,**
Head Basketball Coach, Gonzaga University

"I was going through one of the toughest times of my life, dealing with underlying mental health problems and feeling defeated. Then I met Nick. It's like God placed him in my life just when I needed it the most. We started off with basketball workouts, but then it became bigger than basketball. We would have weekly Bible studies. My faith in God grew, and my game elevated. Not only am I a better player, I'm a better person after meeting Nick. This book reflects who Nick is as a person, and whoever reads this will gain so much from it."

—**Nia Washington,**
Iowa State Women's Basketball

Nick Graham

LUCIDBOOKS

God x Basketball
An Athlete's Playbook to Navigating Life with God's Word

Copyright © 2020 by Nick Graham

Published by Lucid Books in Houston, TX
www.LucidBooksPublishing.com

All rights reserved. No part of this publication may be reproduced, stored in a retrieval system, or transmitted in any form by any means, electronic, mechanical, photocopy, recording, or otherwise, without the prior permission of the publisher, except as provided for by USA copyright law.

Scripture quotations marked (AMP) are taken from the Amplified® Bible (AMP), Copyright © 2015 by The Lockman Foundation. Used by permission. www.Lockman.org

Scripture quotations marked (ESV) are taken from the ESV® Bible (The Holy Bible, English Standard Version®), copyright © 2001 by Crossway, a publishing ministry of Good News Publishers. Used by permission. All rights reserved.

Scripture quotations marked (MSG) are taken from *THE MESSAGE*, copyright © 1993, 1994, 1995, 1996, 2000, 2001, 2002 by Eugene H. Peterson. Used by permission of NavPress. All rights reserved. Represented by Tyndale House Publishers, Inc.

Scripture quotations marked (NIV) are taken from the Holy Bible, New International Version®, NIV®. Copyright ©1973, 1978, 1984, 2011 by Biblica, Inc.™ Used by permission of Zondervan. All rights reserved worldwide. www.zondervan.com The "NIV" and "New International Version" are trademarks registered in the United States Patent and Trademark Office by Biblica, Inc.™

Scripture quotations marked (NKJV) are taken from the New King James Version®. Copyright © 1982 by Thomas Nelson. Used by permission. All rights reserved.

Scripture quotations marked (NLT) are taken from the Holy Bible, New Living Translation, copyright ©1996, 2004, 2007, 2013, 2015 by Tyndale House Foundation. Used by permission of Tyndale House Publishers, Inc., Carol Stream, Illinois 60188. All rights reserved.

Scripture quotations marked (NLV) are taken from the New Life Version, copyright © 1969 and 2003. Used by permission of Barbour Publishing, Inc., Uhrichsville, Ohio 44683. All rights reserved.

ISBN: 978-1-63296-400-7
eISBN: 978-1-63296-399-4

Special Sales: Most Lucid Books titles are available in special quantity discounts. Custom imprinting or excerpting can also be done to fit special needs. Contact Lucid Books at Info@LucidBooksPublishing.com.

Dedicated to the roots of basketball—a game that was created in the spirit of fellowship to develop character and win souls for God.

TABLE OF CONTENTS

Foreword — xvii

Introduction — 1

Devotionals

Prepare for the W — 9
    Soundtrack: "I Can't Lose" – Lecrae & Zaytoven (feat. 24hrs)

God's Recipe Ain't Always Sweet — 13
    Soundtrack: "Just for Me" – Kirk Franklin

God Swag (Part I) — 17
    Soundtrack: "Holy Water" – Lecrae & Zaytoven

Get to Know Your Bucket-Getter (God Swag Part II) — 21
    Soundtrack: "Won't He Do It" – Koryn Hawthorne

Godfidence > Self-Confidence — 25
    Soundtrack: "I'm Blessed" – Charlie Wilson

Focus on Your Target, Not the Dummy D — 29
    Soundtrack: "I'm Getting Ready" – Tasha Cobbs Leonard (feat. Nicki Minaj)

Hit the Showers — 33
    Soundtrack: "Smile" – Tedashii

Walk Around Like You Have an S on Your Chest — 37
    Soundtrack: "Worth" – Anthony Brown & group therAPy

Some Reach, but Few Sustain Greatness — 41
    Soundtrack: "Cycles" – Jonathan McReynolds

Success Is the Test — 45
    Soundtrack: "BlessUp" – Jor'Dan Armstrong

God's Plan — 49
    Soundtrack: "I Know God" – Dee-1

The Big Paint Protector — 53
    Soundtrack: "Fight for Me" – GAWVI (feat. Lecrae)

Follow the Leader 57
    Soundtrack: "TEAM" – Andy Mineo & Wordsplayed (feat. BEAM)

Motivation Monday > Thirsty Thursday 63
    Soundtrack: "123 Victory Remix" – Kirk Franklin (feat. Pharrell Williams)

Play the Hand You're Dealt 67
    Soundtrack: "I Got That (Remix)" – Anthony Brown & group therAPy (feat. 1K Phew)

Break the Press, Beat the Blitz 71
    Soundtrack: "Unstoppable" – Koryn Hawthorne (feat. Yella Beezy)

Live through Him 75
    Soundtrack: "Known" – Tauren Wells

Good Ain't Good Enough 79
    Soundtrack: "Came Up" – Jor'Dan Armstrong

Cultivate Strengths, Eliminate Weaknesses 83
    Soundtrack: "Love Theory" – Kirk Franklin

Put the Ball in God's Hands 87
    Soundtrack: "So Much Luv" – Jor'Dan Armstrong

Growing Pains 91
    Soundtrack: "Pain" – 1K Phew

Be Aggressive or Lose the Lead 95
    Soundtrack: "Put Me In Coach" – Dee-1

Unseen Hours 99
    Soundtrack: "Dreamin'" – Justin Matthew

Where My Real Friends At? 103
    Soundtrack: "Friends" – Andy Mineo

Hold Onto Your How 107
    Soundtrack: "Drown" – Lecrae (feat. John Legend)

Lose Your How, Lose Your Spot (Part I) 111
    Soundtrack: "Real" – Anthony Brown & group therAPy (feat. Jonathan McReynolds)

Lose Your How, Lose Your Spot (Part II) 115
    Soundtrack: "No Gray" – Jonathan McReynolds

Rock Solid 121
    Soundtrack: "The Narrow Road" – Dee-1(feat. Christon Gray)

Know-It-Alls Always Fail 125
    Soundtrack: "Follow the Drip" – Davies

Make It Rain (Like Elijah) 129
    Soundtrack: "God's Got a Blessing" – Norman Hutchins

Internal Drive Leads to External Success 133
    Soundtrack: "Yes You Can" – Marvin Sapp

Stop Settling: Bad Shots Will Get You Beat on and off the Court 137
    Soundtrack: "Blessings" – Lecrae (feat. Ty Dolla $ign)

Keep That Same Energy 141
    Soundtrack: "Oh Lord" – NF

I'm Gonna Need That Same Energy 145
    Soundtrack: "Awesome Remix" – Canton Jones

He Sees It in You 149
    Soundtrack: "The Best in Me" – Marvin Sapp

Dream-Chasing: Catching All God's Goals 153
    Soundtrack: "Way Up (G.O.M. Remix)" – Bizzle (feat. Datin, Selah the Corner, Bumps INF, and Jered Sanders)

Yesterday's Ceiling Is Tomorrow's Floor 157
    Soundtrack: "For the Better" – Bizzle

Follow Through with Faith 161
    Soundtrack: "Do It Again" – Elevation Collective (feat. Travis Greene and Kierra Sheard)

Change the Temperature—Don't Just Check It 165
    Soundtrack: "Light Shine Bright" – TobyMac (feat. Hollyn)

Don't Just Secure the Bag—Share It 169
    Soundtrack: "Bless Up" – Koryn Hawthorne

Represent 173
    Soundtrack: "Never Would Have Made It" – Teyana Taylor

Let God Book Your Flight 177
    Soundtrack: "My God" – J. Monty

Close What's Draining Your Battery — 181
   Soundtrack: "Come With Us" – Deraj (feat. nobigdyl. & BreeKay)

Don't Get Big-Headed — 185
   Soundtrack: "By Chance" – Lecrae & Zaytoven (feat. Verse Simmonds)

Straight Facts, No Gas — 189
   Soundtrack: "BlessUp" – Jor'Dan Armstrong

You Can Have It Your Way — 193
   Soundtrack: "Changed" – Snoop Dogg (feat. Issac Carree & Jazze Pha)

Use Your T.O.s — 197
   Soundtrack: "Fight for Me" – GAWVI (feat. Lecrae)

God's Vision > The Big Picture — 201
   Soundtrack: "Set Me Free" – Lecrae, YK Osiris

Build the Foundation — 205
   Soundtrack: "I'll Find You" – Lecrae (feat. Tori Kelly)

Don't Be a Paint-Job Guy — 209
   Soundtrack: "Deep End" – Lecrae

Hit the Reset Button — 213
   Soundtrack: "I Am a Winner" – Jekalyn Carr

Overtime

You're Dropping Dimes for God, and You Ain't Even Know It — 221

Culture Contract — 223

Keep Going — 225

Someone Needs You Today — 229

Game-Day Challenge — 231

Acknowledgments — 235

FOREWORD

My friendship with Nick Graham is one of my very favorites. At first, ours was a relationship in passing. In the early-to-mid 2000s, when Nick's dad, Paul, was an assistant coach at the University of Colorado, Nick was there every so often, hanging around like kids of most coaches do. Nick was fairly fresh out of college, in search of life's next big thing. Back then, I was covering the University of Colorado Buffaloes men's basketball team as a cub sports reporter for the *Daily Camera* newspaper in Boulder, Colorado.

A few years later, a pickup game invitation from a mutual friend brought us back into the same space.

Then, food.

An invitation to come and break bread with Nick and his friends was the start. He was fun—the kind of guy who could good-naturedly rib anyone, who found joy in connecting people and never compromised any piece of himself to do it.

We talked.

We talked about anything and everything. Long after the party crowds were gone on any particular weekend, there we'd be on an apartment patio trying to solve life's biggest problems. I miss those days. I have told him so. But here's the thing: I had never known how connected to his faith he was, how much that faith guided him daily, how heavily he leaned on it through good and bad times until those talks. It's the kind of thing you wouldn't necessarily know unless you knew him.

Those who knew him did. When one of Nick's good friends decided to get married, he asked Nick to be the officiant. Nick was not only the person who'd engage you in deep conversations about faith, but he was the person you might want to officiate your wedding after you were, well, engaged.

This book, I think, was inevitable.

His life has brought him to this point. He was raised in a house of faith and basketball. He played college basketball in a power conference, the Pac 10 at the time at Washington State, for his father who was the head coach, and went through the ups and downs of being a student athlete. His sister played and coached basketball. Nick coached basketball. Now, he trains young men and women to be better basketball players. Faith and basketball are the woven threads of the tapestry of his life.

He'd have Bible studies with some of the players he trained. He cared about their development as people every bit as much as he cared about their development as basketball players. In my opinion, it was when that was clarified in his mind that this project showed up on his future radar screen, even if he hadn't quite seen it at the time. And it was also at that moment that a previous goal of his—to be a traditional basketball coach—died.

But this is bigger than that. Immensely.

We live in an age when athletes are connecting back to themselves more than ever. They are not shy about publicly sharing their hopes and their fears, discussing their triumphs and shortcomings, and doing it all while reminding the fans who love them that they are more than just players. It is the most 360-degree view of them we've ever had. It started with the athletes viewing themselves in the most holistic manner they ever have.

Nick underwent the same type of metamorphosis. Of course, he wanted to play, and play at the highest level. Of course, he wanted to coach, and coach at the highest level possible. But was he just a player? Was he just a coach? Of course not. More tugged at him.

He looks at this project, at this turn in his life, as a calling. Perhaps he's right. Me? I think this was always what he was born to do. So for him, he had to go through a trying college basketball experience. He had to reach personal milestones and then learn how to graciously and skillfully

FOREWORD

handle them. He had to start a basketball training company and work with everyone from the youngest, most wide-eyed beginners to professionals such as North Carolina and former Denver Nuggets standout Ty Lawson. He had to be encouraged by big camp turnouts and disappointed by things going awry behind the scenes. He had to struggle to keep a car. He had to sleep in one, as well. He had to worry about making rent. He had to experience the joy of getting a college coaching gig in player development at Iowa State, with the frustration of what working there was doing to his psyche—damaging it.

And that's when he started writing. For real. It was therapeutic. He found out those words could be for others, too.

In 22 years as a sports writer and now NBA basketball analyst, I've not encountered many people in the athletic world as grounded and thoughtful as Nick. I've written a feature about him for the *Denver Post*. He's been featured on television, as well.

He's said something to me at various times over the years. I saved the latest iteration when we discussed this book. I've always loved it.

Nick said, "The best thing for me was my ability to be a mentor and help young basketball players develop their character. Because the thing for me is I am very driven to help someone develop as a basketball player. But my challenge for myself, and what I feel like God has called on me to do, is never let their talent supersede their character."

It's that simple in a complex world—saying thank you when a parent goes out of their way to bring you the water bottle you forgot at home; going the extra mile to make sure fans, who spent hard-earned money and may have driven hours to watch you play, feel appreciated; and developing into the best player possible. And at the foundation of it all, putting God at the head of the table.

Nick describes himself as a matchmaker. Swipe left, let God in, see where it goes.

"You get to meet him," he says. "You spend time with him. That's kind of the spirit of the book."

—Christopher Dempsey

INTRODUCTION

Lately, it seems like everyone is collaborating—Nike x Off-White, Supreme x Louis Vuitton, Drake x Migos. I know I'm biased, but none of these even come close to being the best collaboration of all time.

When I first started working in the player development industry 11 years ago, my goal was the same as it is today: to use basketball as a vehicle to fellowship with others, glorify God, and influence others to invest in a personal relationship with God through Jesus Christ. Early on in my career in player development, I received an email from a colleague who expressed his disgust with me for bringing my "Jesus crusade" to the basketball court. He felt that basketball was not a pulpit and that it was not the proper place to promote God. (I've never been one to bully my beliefs on anyone, but I am not afraid to express my love for Jesus and His love for me.)

Basketball had been extremely good to this colleague. He was a standout high school player who had won multiple national titles in college and, at the time of his email, was able to make a good living teaching the game of basketball. But what's ironic is that basketball is God's game—if not for God, there would be no basketball.

James Naismith invented the game of basketball in 1891. His motives for inventing basketball were to keep young men active during the cold winter and use basketball as a vehicle "to win men for the Master through the gym."[1] He felt that "he could better exemplify the Christian life through sports than in the pulpit."[2] I struggle to find any words to describe the love I feel from God to know that He had a plan for you and me—a plan to speak to us, teach us, and love us through the precious game of basketball.

Because basketball has not only impacted me but so many others, I have no choice but to conclude that the best collaboration ever is God x basketball. God gave Naismith a vision to invent a game that would help young people get to know Him, so whenever you bring your faith into basketball, you are staying true to the game and ensuring that the most important colab ever lives on. I am forever grateful, I am honored, and I am obligated to continue the God x basketball collaboration through this book, and I hope and pray that God will touch you to contribute to His culture, as well.

This book is ideal for all of us who love God, want to get to know Him better, and also have a passion for basketball. For those of us who are currently coaching and playing or who are members of a team, here are some specific ways you can read and use this book:

Team Devotional and Discussion

As a group, your team can listen to the soundtrack and then read and discuss the devotional before or after practice or on game day.

Game-Day Devotional

Individually, you can make reading a devotional part of your game-day routine.

Off-Season Character Development Plan

During the off-season, players have a regimented, on-court skill development plan. Reading a devotional daily could serve as your plan for developing your Christlike character.

---

1. Ed Hird, "Dr. James Naismith: Father of Basketball," *EdHird's Blog*, April 25, 2010, https://edhird.com/2010/04/25/dr-james-naismith-father-of-basketball/.
2. "Ordained by God?" *Salvation Basketball*, http://www.salvationbasketball.com/about/was-basketball-ordained-by-god/.

INTRODUCTION

In-Season Perspective Plan

Playing hoops at a high level is extremely demanding in season. The emotional roller coaster of highs and lows often makes it challenging to maintain a proper perspective. By devoting time daily or weekly to read a devotional, you can use this book to ensure you keep a godly perspective during the season.

Pre-Practice

For some athletes, practice provides crippling anxiety that prevents them from enjoying God's gift of competition. Others lose focus on their why, going through the motions and falling short. By reading a devotional before practice, players can be God-led during practice and realize that God has a plan for them both on the court and off.

Morning or Nightly Devotional

It's easy to lose focus on God while we are entrenched in our athletic careers. By making time daily, you will allow God to lead and protect you during your journey.

You'll find the following sections in the devotionals.

Bible Verse

The purpose of this book is to use basketball and sports as a tool to better understand God's Word, which will allow us to connect to God on a much more personal level. Each devotional leads with at least one Bible verse. If you are new to or inexperienced in using the Bible, don't sweat it. There are different translations of the Bible. The translations used for each passage throughout this book are indicated after the verse. These are translations that are easier for Bible newcomers to comprehend. I'd suggest downloading a Bible app that allows you to access most translations. When there are verses that really move me or verses I struggle to comprehend, I use the app to read other translations of the verses.

I'd suggest that when you have time, go back and read the entire chapter of the chosen verse in order to better understand the context of the selected passage.

Soundtrack

Each devotional is paired with a song. Like many of you, I grew up in the hip-hop culture. The selected songs use hip-hop-influenced Christian music as a vehicle to worship God and meditate on His Word.

Visit Godxbasketball.com to download the soundtrack.

And 1

After each devotional, there are points to ponder, and since we are all subscribers of hoop culture, we call them *And 1s*.

Each And 1 is a sticking point that should stay with you. I suggest you begin a God x Basketball journal or start a God x Basketball section of notes on your smartphone.

Drop a Dime

As followers of God, we should strive to be selfless and caring teammates both on the court and off. As we grow in our faith and understanding of who God is, we should not use this relationship to help only ourselves but instead "drop a dime" and assist our teammates, as well. Each devotional calls for you to drop a dime to a friend or teammate.

Overtime

This section at the end of the book includes resources for you to use throughout your life and athletic journey. Don't wait until you finish reading to use them.

God x Basketball

Promote His culture.
Ignite His culture.
Be His culture.
Do it for His culture.

DEVOTIONALS

PREPARE FOR THE W

SOUNDTRACK: "I CAN'T LOSE" – LECRAE & ZAYTOVEN (FEAT. 24HRS)

> *The thief comes only to steal and kill and destroy; I have come that they may have life, and have it to the full.*
> —John 10:10 NIV

> *Therefore submit to God. Resist the devil and he will flee from you.*
> —James 4:7 NKJV

Our toughest opponent isn't on a basketball court. Our toughest opponent is the devil. He is in relentless pursuit of stealing, killing, and destroying everything we have worked for, everything we have, and all we are capable of having in the future.

Proper preparation for a tough opponent is nothing new for athletes. We know that the more challenging the opponent, the more vital preparation becomes. When I was part of the coaching staff at Iowa State during the 2017–2018 season, our preparation heightened whenever we played Kansas. As a team, we understood that we had no chance to win without focused preparation. Kansas was a top-five nationally ranked team that went to the Final Four that season. It has one of the most intimidating home courts in the country.

When preparing to face an opponent capable of not only defeating but embarrassing you, you prepare accordingly if you are committed to winning. That mindset applies to us as we compete against the devil. Just as our team did when preparing to go into enemy territory at Kansas, we also have to acknowledge that the devil is good at what he does and will destroy us if we aren't locked into God's plan. In hoops, our coaches watch film and prepare a scouting report. When the coach prepares the team to face a strong opponent, he will forewarn the players that they have their work cut out for them. He will explain to the team that if they don't lock in and prepare, they will take an L. In John 10:10, Jesus does the same thing—warns us what we are up against when He says the devil is out to ruin us.

For road games, we always met for dinner the evening before the game to go over our scouting report and watch game film. After dissecting the film and identifying how the opposing team would attempt to attack us, one of the coaches at Iowa State would confidently say, "Now let me tell you how we are going to kick their A&%." Obviously, he had to keep it real and let the team know how difficult the challenge would be, but because he wanted the team to trust in the game plan, he always finished with the recipe to defeat the enemy.

While our basketball coaches are good and do their best to prepare us, they aren't always able to provide us with the game-winning scouting report, which was the case when we played against Kansas. We fought hard and came close but took an L. The good news for us in our walk with God is that when He has the scout, He is undefeated. He has never lost, and much like the coach at Iowa State, God is telling us, minus the cussing, how we are going to kick the devil's butt. All you have to do is "submit . . . to God. Resist the devil, and he will flee from you" (James 4:7 NIV).

We have all been in a locker room after a loss that could have been avoided had we listened to our coach and prepared, and that's no fun. Here's to hoping we never have to experience that feeling again on God's journey for us.

And 1

- ❑ Take a few moments to think about a loss caused by a lack of preparation. Reflect on the feelings of regret and disappointment you had and how they could have been avoided.
- ❑ Now, think about losses suffered in other areas of your life that were caused by a lack of preparation. Reflect on the feelings of regret and disappointment you had and how they could have been avoided.
- ❑ Make a list of what you will do differently moving forward to prevent losses caused by a lack of preparation.

Drop a Dime

- ❑ What will you do moving forward to ensure that those around you are prepared and locked in to overcome the opposition on and off the court?

GOD'S RECIPE AIN'T ALWAYS SWEET

SOUNDTRACK: "JUST FOR ME" – KIRK FRANKLIN

Let perseverance finish its work so that you may be mature and complete, not lacking anything.
—James 1:4 NIV

Recently, one of the players I mentor (we'll call him Brevin) informed me that he needed to find another school. He had just finished his freshman year in which he redshirted. As his mentor, I called to check on him, and as you'd imagine, he was very distraught. He was angry with the coaching staff for choosing to move in a different direction and felt as if they'd given up on him prematurely. While I understood Brevin's frustration with the coach's decision, I also encouraged him to take a moment to realize that this was his flour and not his frosting.

Of the many ingredients that go into a cake, not all of them taste as sweet as frosting, but they are all needed to make the cake complete, including ingredients such as flour. In the same way, God calls for many pleasant ingredients in our recipe. However, they ain't all sweet like frosting, and there are some ingredients that don't taste great by themselves. When those unpleasant periods arise, we must stay committed and allow God to complete His recipe. To reach our potential, we must be finished, "not lacking anything" (James 1:4 NIV).

Brevin is incredibly talented, but even he agreed that he could be more focused, more determined, more humble, and maybe even have more of a chip on his shoulder. In my experience, going through hurtful events such as getting benched or being booed by fans can create a chip on an athlete's shoulder that produces the determination, drive, and motivation to dig deeper and overcome obstacles. We concluded that for Brevin to reach his potential as a player, he needed to equip himself with these attributes.

As you go through your "flour moments," hold onto this truth: Dark days are merely a distasteful but necessary ingredient in God's recipe to allow you to reach your destiny. While we would prefer not to go through them, we have to acknowledge that there's a purpose in pain, and we must trust that today's toughness will be tomorrow's testimony. Flour doesn't taste good, but it's going to make for one heckuva cake.

And 1

- ❏ Reflect on a "flour moment" athletically that was no fun at the moment but something you needed to go through to become a better player.
- ❏ Reflect on a "flour moment" in your walk with God that was no fun at the moment but was something you now realize God allowed you to go through in order to be more prepared for your journey.

Drop a Dime

- ❏ Take a moment to let God lead you to identify someone who needs to know that their tough time is merely a "flour moment" that will be an ingredient to allow them to reach their potential.
- ❏ Ask God to prepare their heart to receive His message of encouragement.
- ❏ Send them a personalized message of encouragement and share this devotional with them.

GOD SWAG (PART I)

SOUNDTRACK: "HOLY WATER" – LECRAE & ZAYTOVEN

> *Then call on the name of your god, and I will call on the name of the LORD. The god who answers by setting fire to the wood is the true God!" And all the people agreed. . . . At the usual time for offering the evening sacrifice, Elijah the prophet walked up to the altar and prayed, "O LORD, God of Abraham, Isaac, and Jacob, prove today that you are God in Israel and that I am your servant. Prove that I have done all this at your command. O LORD, answer me! Answer me so these people will know that you, O LORD, are God and that you have brought them back to yourself." . . . And when all the people saw it, they fell face down on the ground and cried out, "The LORD—he is God! Yes, the LORD is God!"*
> —1 Kings 18:24, 36–37, 39 NLT

I don't think you will find an athlete who would disagree with the notion that to thrive athletically, your swagger must remain on 100. Regardless of ability, if an athlete's swag decreases, so, too, will that athlete's athletic performance. The same can be said for us in everyday life: Without true swag, we will never sustain success and overcome devilish haters.

It's not the smooth seas that determine a good sailor; it's the rough waters. And it's not the times of comfort that expose a person's swagger; it's how they respond in times of uncertainty when their backs are against the wall. As athletes, we know it's easy to have swag in practice when we are in a controlled scrimmage against the second team, but what defines our swag is whether we can maintain it after the last media time-out in a close game against the best team in our league.

In today's verses, Elijah provides us with a vivid example of what swag is. Despite 450 others worshiping Baal, their god, Elijah stood out in faith and trusted that God would answer his prayer. God proved to the doubters that He is the one true God.

I encourage you to read the entire 18th chapter of 1 Kings to truly grasp the confidence and faith Elijah had in God. Here are the takeaways for us from Elijah:

1. Elijah spent enough time with God to hear God's plan for him. When his back was against the wall, he knew that despite overwhelming circumstances, God's plan was bigger.
2. Elijah's motives were for God's purpose to be carried out through him for the good of God's people and not for his selfish desires.
3. Elijah's faith was not in his own ability, in anyone else's ability, or in their god. He placed complete trust in God's plan because he knew God personally, and he knew that God's plan was greater than decimating circumstances.

If we get to know God's plan for our lives and our careers, maintain godly motives, and rely solely on God, we, too, can develop Elijah-like swag.

And 1

- ❑ Identify a time athletically when you or someone you witnessed displayed Elijah-like swagger on the court. Where did the swagger come from?

- ❏ Identify a time off the court when your swag disappeared because you became overwhelmed by your circumstances. What happened to allow your swag to vanish? How would the outcome have been different if you had applied Elijah's three-step plan?
- ❏ Identify a teammate who possesses Elijah-like swagger that can only come from being led by God. Study that person, and determine what habits he or she has that produce that true swagger.

Drop a Dime
- ❏ Pray that God leads you to identify a teammate who needs to hear Elijah's story of knowing God well enough to trust that God's plan is > their overwhelming circumstances. Share this devotional with them.

GET TO KNOW YOUR BUCKET-GETTER (GOD SWAG PART II)

SOUNDTRACK: "WON'T HE DO IT" – KORYN HAWTHORNE

> *At the usual time for offering the evening sacrifice, Elijah the prophet walked up to the altar and prayed, "O LORD, God of Abraham, Isaac, and Jacob, prove today that you are God in Israel and that I am your servant. Prove that I have done all this at your command. O LORD, answer me! Answer me so these people will know that you, O LORD, are God and that you have brought them back to yourself." Immediately the fire of the LORD flashed down from heaven and burned up the young bull, the wood, the stones, and the dust. It even licked up all the water in the trench! And when all the people saw it, they fell face down on the ground and cried out, "The LORD—he is God! Yes, the LORD is God!"*
>
> —1 Kings 18:36–39 NLT

Back when Carmelo Anthony was in Denver and in the prime of his career, I was fortunate to play pick-up with him and some of the other members of the Denver Nuggets. I was on Melo's team, and we ran everybody off the floor, never losing a game.

Having seen Melo play (when I was a spectator), I already knew he was a bucket, but watching him from afar does not give his game proper justice. When you are on the floor playing with him and, in my case, on his team, you develop a different appreciation for his offensive talent.

We led wire-to-wire in some of the games we played and ran the other team off the floor, but in many of the games we played, it appeared we were destined to take an L. Despite coming close to losing, we never did because of Melo. He was so gifted that it mattered not what the defense did; they couldn't stop him from getting a bucket.

As a basketball student and teacher, I had a deep appreciation for Melo's game because of what I had heard and observed, but I had never experienced it as his teammate. With every possession we played together, my confidence in his ability to lead us to victory grew. After a few games when he put us on his back, I developed an unwavering faith in our team's ability to succeed no matter who the opposition was.

Similar to my playing with Melo, Elijah had faith in his ultimate teammate—God. Despite facing what appeared to be a losing situation in the passage from 1 Kings, Elijah knew what God could and would do. He knew that because of what he'd witnessed God do previously. Prior to his adverse situation, he prayed and recalled all God had done. Elijah's swag came from his Savior and gave him the courage to aggressively pursue and expect victory in the face of unbelievers and haters.

Have you drawn close enough to God to witness for yourself what He's capable of doing for you and through you? When you get up close and personal with God, it's just different. It's one thing to read about what He's done and hear from others about how good He is. But until you get close enough to see Him win battles you never knew you could win, you will never realize that He is the Ultimate Bucket. No matter what the enemy does, God will always prevail in your life and career.

And 1

- ❑ Have you drawn close enough to God to witness how marvelous of a teammate He is?
- ❑ Is there an area of your life where you have conceded defeat because it appears the odds are too overwhelming?

GET TO KNOW YOUR BUCKET-GETTER (GOD SWAG PART II)

Drop a Dime

- ❑ Ask God to lead you to the teammate who lacks belief in what God can do through them on the court and in life. Share the passages from this devotional, and assure that player that the same God who was with Elijah is with them, as well.

GODFIDENCE > SELF-CONFIDENCE

SOUNDTRACK: "I'M BLESSED" – CHARLIE WILSON

Jesus looked at them intently and said, "Humanly speaking, it is impossible. But not with God. Everything is possible with God."
—Mark 10:27 NLT

Don't be so naive and self-confident. You're not exempt. You could fall flat on your face as easily as anyone else. Forget about self-confidence; it's useless. Cultivate God-confidence.
—1 Cor. 10:12 MSG

Self-confidence can take you only so far. There will be times in your life and playing career when the challenges you are going through exceed the confidence you have in yourself. During those times, if you don't navigate through life with "Godfidence," you will crumble. Godfidence is confidence on steroids. It's unshakable: No matter how bad things appear, you believe not in yourself but in the God who made you and is with you to overcome all adversity.

I've failed time and time again because I gave myself far too much credit and believed I could navigate through life with self-confidence. For a while, my self-confidence got me by, but when life turned upside down, my swag went out the window, and I was left broken and damaged.

On the other hand, when I relied on Godfidence to navigate through life, it mattered not how hard the devil tried—he couldn't win. Even if I was knocked down in the mud—somehow, someway—God allowed me to get up without leaving so much as a stain on me.

If you are honest with yourself, you, too, can look back and identify the negative results of relying on self-confidence over Godfidence. You probably experienced just enough success to continue to operate in self-confidence and became more dependent on self and less dependent on God. But eventually, you got your starting spot snatched up, had a season-ending injury and lacked the belief you could overcome it, fractured a relationship, or got hit with a financial hardship. You felt helpless and hopeless because, during difficult times such as those, your so-called abundance of self-confidence abandoned you.

As Mark 10:27 states, human possibility and self-confidence have limitations, but through God, what seems to be impossible is possible. If you have lived life long enough and played basketball long enough, you've probably found out the hard way that you can't be all God called you to be in your own confidence. Living life and pursuing a basketball career at the highest levels prove that self-confidence is fickle; it wavers; it's here today and gone tomorrow, but God's swag stays on 100. It has stood the test of time. Only through Godfidence can we live the fulfilling life of destiny God wants us to live on and off the court.

And 1

- ❏ Have you experienced a moment in sports and in life where you crumbled because you relied on self instead of God?
- ❏ If yes, write down the moment (or moments), along with the results of what happened.

- ☐ If no, spend some quiet time with God, and reach out to a spiritual mentor to determine where in your life you need to shift from relying on self-confidence to relying on Godfidence. Once identified, list those areas, and write out a prayer that both you and your mentor can pray daily.

Drop a Dime
- ☐ Help at least one teammate develop Godfidence both on the court and off.

FOCUS ON YOUR TARGET, NOT THE DUMMY D

SOUNDTRACK: "I'M GETTING READY" – TASHA COBBS LEONARD (FEAT. NICKI MINAJ)

> *Do not fret because of those who are evil or be envious of those who do wrong; for like the grass they will soon wither, like green plants they will soon die away. Trust in the L*ORD *and do good; dwell in the land and enjoy safe pasture. Take delight in the L*ORD*, and he will give you the desires of your heart. Commit your way to the L*ORD*; trust in him and he will do this: He will make your righteous reward shine like the dawn, your vindication like the noonday sun.*
>
> —Ps. 37:1–6 NIV

I have battled with anxiety most of my life. I often allow worry to consume my thoughts, and in the past, that worry has manifested into a paralyzing fear that prevented me from living the life God predestined for me to live.

The thing about focus is that you can't focus on two things at once. As a result, the more I focused on worry, the more I lost belief in God's supernatural favor for my life, not because it did not exist but because I did not focus on it. I read somewhere that we ought to gaze at God and glance at our fears. I've had to acknowledge that I was hustling backward. I was so focused on worry that I lost sight of God and how magnificent He is.

During one of our post player development workouts, a player struggled to make his jump hooks. He was more than capable of making the shots since he is an incredibly talented post player. Often, a capable player may not succeed because of a lack of effort, but this player was going as hard as he possibly could. This player had a laser-like focus. Unfortunately, his focus was misplaced.

During the drills, the coach had a blocking pad to provide dummy defense during the players' reps. Dummy defense, or dummy D, is when the coach provides a defensive look and feel. The player knew what the defender was going to do. He knew the coach was going to give him a good bump or two, but the coach was not going to steal the ball, and he wasn't going to block his shot.

After a few misses, the coaches and I noticed that as this player caught the ball and went into his jump hook, he was focused on the dummy defense and not the target. After a few reps, I pulled him to the side and asked him why he looked at the dummy D and not the goal. I then asked him what was important—the dummy D or the target? It made no sense for him to take his eyes off the target to focus on the dummy defender who couldn't steal the ball or block his shot. I suggested he focus on the target. He would still be able to sense the opposition, and he could also see the defender attempting to disrupt him out of his peripheral vision while maintaining focus on what was important.

The player took heed of the advice and refused to compromise, losing focus on what was important in the presence of a distracting defender. He went on to rattle off eight straight jump hooks to finish the drill.

As the drill concluded, I could feel God looking down on me from heaven, making sure I understood that the player wasn't the only one allowing a dummy defender to distract him from what's important.

FOCUS ON YOUR TARGET, NOT THE DUMMY D

As talented as the player was and as hard as he worked, he couldn't succeed when he lost focus. As I continue to grow closer to God, I realize that the same holds true for me. When God created me, He created me to do great things, and if I lose focus, I will not prevail. Instead, I must continue to hold onto God's truth to "take delight in the LORD, and he will give you the desires of your heart" (Ps. 37:4 NIV). Much like the post player, I will then succeed, and the enemy will no longer be able to distract me with worry and anxiety.

And 1

- ❏ List at least three dummy defenders that have distracted you from focusing on God and what God has for you.

Drop a Dime

- ❏ Identify two teammates who could be doing more if they had the proper focus.
- ❏ Every day for the next week, pray for those two teammates to focus on God and not the dummy defenders in their lives.
- ❏ Pray that God prepares you to gently help them get their focus on God and off their problems.
- ❏ Share your breakthrough with us on Twitter @GodxBasketball using the hashtag #focusonyourtarget so we can celebrate what God is doing for and through you.

HIT THE SHOWERS

SOUNDTRACK: "SMILE" – TEDASHII

> *But if we confess our sins to him, he is faithful and just to forgive us our sins and to cleanse us from all wickedness.*
> —1 John 1:9 NLT

One of my college teammates at Washington State hated to take showers. It was not only one of the nastiest things I've experienced but also one of the dumbest. In the Pac-12, you go on conference road trips for up to five days at a time, and that dude would not take a shower the entire trip. There were times when he'd travel back on the plane, still wearing his jersey under his travel sweats after playing more than 30 minutes. We all prayed that we did not have to sit next to him on the plane and attempted to bribe our coaches so we didn't have to room with him on road trips. When we played at home, he'd accumulate so much dirt that he'd sweat a ring of dirt onto his white jersey. He attempted to go the entire Christmas break without taking a shower—keep in mind that we practiced twice a day. The only way we could get him to shower over the break was to withhold his meal money until he showered, and we had to make sure he used soap.

What made no sense was that showers cost him nothing. My fellow teammates and I could not understand why he wouldn't take a shower to cleanse himself of the dirt he was carrying around for days or even weeks at a time. In the locker room, we had an infinite number of towels, soap, hot water, and showers. Instead of taking advantage of washing the dirt off for free, he chose to be dirty, and as a result, people hated to be around him.

Spiritually speaking, I wonder if I am like my dirty teammate, walking around carrying years of dirt unnecessarily. Am I not taking advantage of the free cleansing God provides through Jesus? The price has already been paid for me to cleanse myself of previous filth. We once had three-a-day practices, and after every practice, I was dirty. I got dirty three times, so I took three showers. I didn't just take a shower after the first practice and conclude I had reached my limit of showers for the day. I took advantage of my limitless supply of showers and cleansed myself every time I was filthy.

As a child of God who acknowledges that Jesus paid the price for me to cleanse myself every time I'm dirty, I need to have the same approach I did when we had three practices in one day. Some days I may get dirty 10 times, and if that's the case, I need to wash the dirt off 10 times. God did not say there was a limit to how many times He will forgive us of our sins. I don't know about you, but I choose to take advantage of the unlimited spiritual showers offered through Jesus dying for my sins, and I choose not to live life dirty.

And 1

- ❑ Spiritually speaking, do you walk around like my dirty teammate, or do you spiritually cleanse yourself of dirt by confessing your sins?

Drop a Dime

- ❑ Identify a teammate who needs to realize they don't have to carry their old dirt around. Share this devotional with them.

WALK AROUND LIKE YOU HAVE AN S ON YOUR CHEST

SOUNDTRACK: "WORTH" – ANTHONY BROWN & GROUP THERAPY

> *God can do anything, you know—far more than*
> *you could ever imagine or guess or request in your wildest dreams!*
> *He does it not by pushing us around but by working within us,*
> *his Spirit deeply and gently within us.*
> —Eph. 3:20 MSG

A few seasons ago, one of the players I mentor called me (let's call her Mia). She was very frustrated. A sophomore in college, she felt she never got a fair shake on the court. The assistant coach who recruited her had become a head coach at another school, and Mia felt the current coaches were not fans of her game. The coaches were nice to her off the court, and they weren't disrespectful to her on the court, but they did not invest in coaching her as they did her teammates.

Mia felt invisible. The head coach even went two weeks without speaking to her directly. It wasn't that the coach was upset with Mia—he just forgot about her because he assumed she was ordinary and focused instead on coaching those he felt had extraordinary talent.

My advice to Mia was to never let anyone stop her from walking around with an *S* on her chest. When Superman was Clark Kent, very few treated him the same as they did Superman, but Clark Kent never let that treatment affect how he felt about himself. I wonder why he never lost confidence when others saw him as unassuming, ordinary, and someone to be walked all over. I believe it's because he knew that regardless of how he was treated by others, he was still Superman.

We can learn a lot from Clark Kent. Most of the world will see you for the Clark Kent you appear to be on the exterior. Don't let that discourage you. Just because others do not see and acknowledge the Superman or Superwoman in you does not mean it is not there. If you don't believe me, believe the player I mentored. Mia accepted God's Word and began to practice like she had an S on her chest, watch film like she had an S on her chest, and put in extra work after practice like she had an S on her chest. Then, during a nationally televised game during her team's conference tournament during March Madness, Mia was called on to play extended minutes because of foul trouble. She came off the bench and scored 18 points, hitting the game winner. The team went on to win the championship and advance to the Big Dance, which they would not have done without her.

Ephesians 3:20 promises that we each have the Superhero of all superheroes gently dwelling in us, and when the time is right, the world will see the S on our chests and be blown away. If you hang in with hope, God will help you tap into your superpowers and overcome anyone who doesn't see the Superman or Superwoman in you.

As God anoints you to have your superhero moments in sports and life, don't be surprised by those who jump on your bandwagon. Everyone wants to rock with Superman and Superwoman, but very few will ride or die with Clark Kent. That's okay—do not hold it against them, but know that your humble example opens up the door for God to work through you and help others activate their own superhero.

And 1

- ❑ Identify a time in sports or in another area of your life when someone dismissed your ability to be a difference-maker because they did not see your S.

- ❑ What impact did it have on you, and would you have reacted differently if you had applied Ephesians 3:20 to the situation?
- ❑ Are you prepared the next time others dismiss you? Why or why not?

Drop a Dime
- ❑ Now that you have discovered your superpower, help a teammate recognize theirs. There's someone in your life right now who has believed the lie that they are not special and equipped with God's superpower inside them. Ask God to work through you to convince them that they have a Superhero living inside them.

SOME REACH, BUT FEW SUSTAIN GREATNESS

SOUNDTRACK: "CYCLES" – JONATHAN MCREYNOLDS

You have not chosen Me, I have chosen you. I have set you apart for the work of bringing in fruit. Your fruit should last. And whatever you ask the Father in My name, He will give it to you.

—John 15:16 NLV

If you want to squeeze every ounce of opportunity out of life, don't settle for reaching your goals—commit to sustaining them.

What do you want to do when you get to the mountaintop? Do you want to do all the climbing, grinding, and sacrificing just to reach it, look at the view, and then head back down to the valley? Or once you get there and see the majestic view, do you want to live up there?

As it relates to achieving and sustaining success, there are levels to it. Some will never commit to developing the drive to climb to the top of the mountain, while others will make the climb but do so prematurely. They will forget to pack their commitment, humility, character, conviction, courage, drive, and ability to isolate when needed. As a result, when they reach the mountaintop, they will have to head back down to the valley and hopefully plan better for the future.

It's heartbreaking to witness players sacrifice family time, social life, and vacations in order to reach their goal briefly, only to lose it all and have to start from scratch. Unfortunately, I have seen this scene more than a few times. As a trainer, I've worked with a few players who conquered the unimaginable and achieved their lifelong goal of making it to the league, only to have the visit to their mountaintop end early because they forgot to pack.

Prior to beginning any journey, you need to understand that the longer you plan on staying, the more time it will take you to prepare before you begin. In addition, the longer you plan to stay, the more expensive the trip will be. If you were going on a day trip, you wouldn't need to check a bag, it wouldn't take you long to pack, and the cost of the trip would be minimal. If you were going to a destination for a week, you'd have to devote more time to packing, and you'd have to pay to check a bag. If you planned on moving and never coming back, you'd have to be prepared for the considerable time commitment required to pack, and you'd also have to pay for the move to your new residence.

The same holds true for life—if you plan on moving to your mountaintop and never coming back, you have to pay the price and put in time before you even make the climb. Like any other move, you have to figure out what you are going to keep and what you are going to discard. You can't keep everything.

We already identified what needs to accompany us on the move, so now let's determine what we need to leave behind—inconsistency, excuses, jealousy, expectations of others, shortcuts, blaming others, settling for less than our best, and anything else you can think of that will weigh you down. Once you decide to relocate to the mountaintop, never compare your move to others. They may, indeed, be moving faster up the mountain than you are, and comparing yourself will only discourage you. But what you have to realize is that they may be going only for a quick visit and, therefore, they may not have to take the time to prepare and pack like you did.

If you are going to squeeze every ounce of opportunity out of life, don't settle for reaching your goals—commit to sustaining them. Now that you know how long you want to go, pack accordingly, and keep in mind that Jesus chose us to remain on the mountaintop. John 15:16 tells us that Jesus did not choose us to have one great season and then go back to being average. No, He says something like this: "I selected you long before you chose Me to win through My power and for My purposes, continually for the rest of your life." He has equipped us and expects us to WIN, WIN, WIN, WIN (Jay Rock voice)!

And 1

- ❏ Write down what you need to pack before you commit to climbing the mountaintop God has for you.
- ❏ Write down what you need to leave behind before you commit to climbing the mountaintop God has for you.

Drop a Dime

- ❏ Identify at least one teammate who needs to make sure they are adequately packed for their climb.
- ❏ Allow God to work through you to help them make a list of what needs to be packed and what needs to be left behind.

SUCCESS IS THE TEST

SOUNDTRACK: "BLESSUP" — JOR'DAN ARMSTRONG

For all those who exalt themselves will be humbled, and those who humble themselves will be exalted.

—Luke 14:11 NIV

God wants to gently humble us on the front end so we don't have to go through the embarrassment of losing His blessings publicly. While being humbled is not fun, it is necessary, and even when you obey God's will, He will allow seasons of humility into your life. These seasons are not punishment but preparation for the test.

God doesn't want us to have blessings without first having character. A lack of character leads to an ego—and egos trip, but the humble don't stumble. One weekend in particular during my freshman year in college, I played and won a Saturday afternoon game where I hit my career high. Every college player knows you want to play well at Saturday home games, so you can get gassed up at all the parties at night. (Be careful about the gas you take in—all gas ain't good gas. Praise that is just surface level leads to getting a big head and losing your humility.)

To say I was feeling myself would have been an understatement. I went to all the parties that night and basked in the praise I got from everyone. I had just started dating my college girlfriend, who was with me at the parties, and let's just say I was a little too cordial to all the other girls who were congratulating me. My girlfriend rightfully wasn't too happy and gave me the silent treatment for a week after that.

I assumed the rest of the season was "gonna be a breeze, big fella." But our next game was the following Tuesday, and I played like crap, got benched, and had no one to blame but myself. I was the same person who had dominated a few days prior—the difference was that my hunger and humility were replaced with an inflated ego, and I stumbled. I wasn't prepared for success, leading to a missed opportunity to improve, lost playing time, and an upset girlfriend.

If you aren't careful, success can be your most significant distraction. Like many college athletes, I struggled to balance my faith, athletics, academics, and social life. If I'm honest with myself, my faith was the least of my worries. The result of my lack of commitment to my faith was that God couldn't gently humble me and, in turn, help sustain my success. My lack of humility on the front end led to my being humbled in front of thousands on the back end. In the words of my close friend and mentor Chauncey Billups, "Sometimes success is the test." If that's the case, then humility is the answer, as stated in Luke 14:11.

And 1

- ❏ Reflect on a time when you did not allow God to humble you before He blessed you, and as a result you didn't pass the test of success.
- ❏ List what you would do differently if you had it to do over.
- ❏ Identify at least two ways God is trying to humble you.

Drop a Dime

- ❏ Identify a teammate you feel needs to allow God to humble them so they can pass the test of success.
- ❏ Pray for them every day for the next week.

- ❏ Share with them your personal story of when you did not allow God to humble you before the test, and mention the negative result it produced.
- ❏ Ask them if they will allow you to help them identify how God is attempting to humble them.

GOD'S PLAN

SOUNDTRACK: "I KNOW GOD" — DEE-1

"For I know the plans I have for you," declares the LORD,
"plans to prosper you and not to harm you,
plans to give you hope and a future."
—Jer. 29:11 NIV

He replied, "Because you have so little faith. Truly I tell you,
if you have faith as small as a mustard seed, you can say to this
mountain, 'Move from here to there,' and it will move.
Nothing will be impossible for you."
—Matt. 17:20 NIV

One of the players I work with needed to develop a floater. The process of developing a floater for this player, like others, began as a painful process. When we started, he looked terrible, felt terrible, and was frequently frustrated. Despite his frustration, his hope and trust in me as his trainer fueled him to stay committed to the process.

His commitment allowed him to develop a fluid floater that he, his coaches, and his teammates could be confident in. During one significant game, he caught the ball off a reversal and made a hard baseline drive, and as the help defender rotated over, he quickly set his feet and swished a floater. He could take advantage of this big moment because he did not reject the plan I had for his game. He trusted me because he knew my resume for developing players. My previous success gave him faith that even when he had moments of doubt and assumed he'd never be able to add a floater to his bag, he could trust me.

As Christ-followers, we can learn a lot from that player. If he could have faith in my plan, we ought to have no problem trusting God because His resume speaks for itself. God tells us in Matthew 17:20 that through His power and for His purposes, we can move mountains. Factor that in with the fact that He has a detailed plan specifically for us, and we should have no reservations.

To help you chase down your dreams and pursue excellence, God will often bless you with a process of pain that gives birth to His blessings. We all have huge dreams, but if we are honest with ourselves, we have no idea how to navigate from where we are now to arrive at those dreams. But God does, because He's the one who placed those dreams in our hearts in the first place. God is not a mean-spirited God merely taking our dreams and dangling them over us like a carrot. Jeremiah 29:11 states that God has a detailed plan of action to lead us toward our big dreams. He knows that days of difficulty, days of doubt, and days of despair stand between us and our big dreams in basketball and every other area of our lives. God provides us comfort and confidence through Jeremiah 29:11 in such times of turbulence.

No different from the player I developed who needed to create a floater, we have to let God develop skills in us so we can be all we can for Him and achieve our big dreams through His power and for His purposes.

And 1

- ❑ What skills is God trying to develop in you to prepare you for your big moment?

- ❑ Reflect on a time when you had to place blind faith in a coach to level up athletically.
- ❑ Does that experience help you make sense of being prepared to trust God to level you up spiritually? How?

Drop a Dime

- ❑ Ask God to reveal to you a teammate who may not realize that their current period of discomfort is part of God's plan for their growth.
- ❑ Once you identify that teammate, send them an encouraging text message and continue to support them until they buy into God's plan for their life.

THE BIG PAINT PROTECTOR

SOUNDTRACK: "FIGHT FOR ME" – GAWVI (FEAT. LECRAE)

> *For the angel of the Lord is a guard; he surrounds and defends all who fear him.*
> —Ps. 34:7 NLT

Regardless of the type of defense you're playing and the defensive principles you value, it's never a good thing if you allow the opposition to live in the paint. If they frequently visit your paint, chances are you will be going home with an L. On the other hand, if you can keep them out of the heart of your defense, you should prevail. God loves us so much that He protects our paint if we allow Him to. In the past, I've been stubborn and attempted to protect the paint in my power and strength as opposed to funneling enemies and haters to God—and that never ended well.

Psalm 34:7 states that God has sent angels down to protect our paint. My walk with Christ is similar to my career in college—I tried hard, but I was frequently too thin to win. I'm only five feet eleven, which means I'm undersized for basketball. I was not equipped to protect the paint when guarding bigger players who overpowered me and scored over me.

My college team had no paint protectors, so I just had to take my Ls. In my journey to God's destiny for my life, though, I have the Ultimate Paint Protector. I had to realize that when life overpowers me, all I need to do is force it to my Help. If we allow God to, He will not let anything get to the heart. He will protect the paint better than Shaq, Rudy Gobert, Joel Embiid, JaVale McGee, or any of the other great paint protectors.

The good thing about good help is that even when you cannot see it, you know it's there. While I focus on the task at hand and feel overmatched, my Help yells at me and lets me know, "I got help behind you; just send 'em to me." The good news is that God has not given up one paint touch my entire life. Every player knows that their swag is different when they are on the floor with a paint protector, not because of their ability but because of the ability of the paint protection behind them. The protector takes the pressure off them to handle defense on their own, just as God defends you in your journey toward greatness.

And 1

- ❑ As players, we all know that playing with a paint protector takes pressure off us. How can allowing God to do the heavy lifting in your life take pressure off you?
- ❑ Reflect on a time when you relied on your own strength to overcome overwhelming adversity instead of letting God take the lead. What was the result?

Drop a Dime

- ❑ Identify a teammate attempting to overcome adversity in their own power instead of funneling the adversity to God.
- ❑ List three ways they can give God their problems.
- ❑ Pray that God prepares them to receive His message, and pray for God to speak through you in a loving, gentle, and encouraging way.
- ❑ Share this message and your list with your teammate.

FOLLOW THE LEADER

SOUNDTRACK: "TEAM" — ANDY MINEO & WORDSPLAYED (FEAT. BEAM)

Become wise by walking with the wise; hang out with fools and watch your life fall to pieces.
—Prov. 13:20 MSG

As you make your way to where you are going, be careful who you get directions from, because there's no way to get to the right place if you are listening to the wrong people.[1]

Too often, we look up to those who do not have a good role model to look up to themselves. Before we look up to someone, we ought to see what or who it is they look up to. For me, I choose only to look up to those who have surrendered to God's calling in their lives. As a result, God is alive and working in and through them, which means they are not influencing me but the God in them is.

---

1. Frederick Haynes III, "Where You Are Going Ain't on the Map," sermon preached January 14, 2018, at Friendship-West Baptist Church, Dallas, Texas.

It'd be a shame for you to work hard but never succeed because you didn't allow God to lead you to the right role models. If we select leaders to follow on our own, we could fall victim to following a fraudulent leader who could lead us away from the direction we hope to go and, more importantly, the direction God designed for us to go. If we allow God to lead us toward godly mentors, we won't grind and sacrifice only to realize that despite being well-intentioned, we went the wrong way.

They say your decisions determine your destiny. It seems like the more I allow godly mentors to influence me, the more success I experience. Here are a few of my godly mentors in basketball, along with the reasons they're on my team. I like to call them my God Squad.

Team Captain
Paul Graham, my dad, is without question the toughest dude on the planet. Life dealt him a bad hand. He grew up poor, parentless, and black in the '60s. He grew up being laughed at and told he would never amount to anything. Through his faith in God, he graduated from college as a world-class hurdler in track and field. After college, he reunited with the sport he loved—basketball. Dad began his coaching career at Kimball High School in Dallas and turned the team into a powerhouse. He started his college career in 1982 at SMU, back when discrimination against black coaches was a frequent practice. Despite being regarded as one of the top assistant coaches in the country, he was frequently overlooked for head coaching jobs because of the color of his skin.

I saw firsthand when life delivered my dad knockout blows, frequently bringing him to tears. On more than one occasion, he was told directly by institutions that they would not hire him because of his race. But no matter how many tears he cried and how hard he got knocked down, he never lost his faith in God's plan for his life, and he never stopped fighting. He is my personal example that with God, you can crash through glass ceilings and break through closed doors. After 17 years of knockdowns as Dad pursued his dream of becoming a Division 1 college basketball coach, God led him to achieve that dream in the spring of 1999 at Washington State. My dad went from the projects of Kansas City during segregation to earning undergraduate and master's degrees, to overcoming discrimination and being an African American head coach at a Power-5 school. He influenced me to have this same faith and to fight with God's power, and this example is why he is the team captain of my God Squad.

Starting Five (plus 1—there's no way I could leave one of these men off this list)

Tony Bennett is the head coach of the 2019 national champion Virginia Cavaliers. He is a Christ-led coach not just with words but with actions, as well. The foundation of his program is built on Christian principles—humility, passion, unity, servanthood, and thankfulness. As it relates to servanthood, Bennett put his money where his mouth was. He was offered a substantial raise and turned it down. Instead, he asked that the money be applied toward not only his program but other athletic programs at the university.

Carlos Daniel of the Denver Nuggets lives a Christ-led life despite working in a profession where many assume it's impossible to do so. He is never afraid to tell me the truth in love and holds me accountable to be the best version of myself. For his sacrifice, he has earned the right to lead me.

Ricardo Patton (@coachrpatton) is an assistant coach at Vanderbilt. He has sustained success as a head coach at the high-major level and has never compromised his faith in God for professional gain.

Melvin Hunt (@mhuntnba314) is an assistant coach for the Atlanta Hawks. Melvin has always glorified God in all he does as a basketball coach and uses his platform to serve others.

Chauncey Billups (@1MrBigShot) is an NBA champion and current ESPN NBA analyst. Chauncey has provided me with a first-class example of how to remain humble and grounded while receiving God's blessings. Chauncey frequently speaks greatness into me and inspires me to do the same for those who look up to me.

Rod Barnes (@CoachRodBarnes) is the head coach at Cal State Bakersfield. His resume speaks for itself. He was selected as the AP National Coach of the Year in 2001 and the National Mid-Major Coach of the Year in 2017. He's succeeded at the highest level while never compromising God's calling on his career. He's shown me that you can succeed and keep God first, which is why he's on my team.

We had the game right when we were kids—we played follow the leader, not follow the follower. Often, we miss the boat and condemn followers. There's nothing wrong with being a follower; in fact, I am able to succeed because I follow my Lord and Savior and my squad. We all need directions to reach our destiny. The question you must honestly answer is this: Do you have trusted leaders to give you direction?

And 1

- ❑ Remember, before you look up to someone, examine who they look up to. Determine whether they are consistent and obedient in who they follow. Are you able to identify the godly leaders in your life? How?
- ❑ Take a moment and surrender to God. Ask Him to reveal who should lead you and to point out anyone who's leading you away from His promises. Ask God to give you the courage to walk away from ungodly leadership and replace it with your God Squad.
- ❑ List your God Squad starting five, and provide at least one reason why they are on the team. I'll start your list off for you.

Owner – God

General Manager – Jesus

Head Coach – The Holy Spirit

Starting 5:

1.

2.

3.

4.

5.

Drop a Dime:
- ❑ Take a moment and send your God Squad a handwritten note, email, or text message. Let them know why you appreciate their significant contribution to your development.
- ❑ Shout out your squad on Twitter with the hashtag #GodSquad and @ us @cultureirdie @godxbasketball.

MOTIVATION MONDAY >
THIRSTY THURSDAY

SOUNDTRACK: "123 VICTORY REMIX" – KIRK FRANKLIN (FEAT. PHARRELL WILLIAMS)

> *Watch out for the Esau syndrome: trading away God's lifelong gift in order to satisfy a short-term appetite.*
> —Heb. 12:16 MSG

> *The road to success is dotted with many tempting parking spaces.*
> —Will Rogers

When you decide to go on a journey, you must never lose sight of the destination. Your destination drives you and keeps you focused on what matters most. Hebrews 12:16 explains that Esau gave away his inheritance because he was hungry, and his temporary pains of hunger shifted his focus from his long-term well-being to satisfying his appetite in the short term.

I can relate to Esau. I once missed my connecting flight because the airport where I was laid over had a Pappadeaux—my favorite restaurant. Despite being pressed for time, I decided to eat there during my layover. Just like Esau, I lost focus on what mattered most and missed my flight.

The obvious takeaway is to focus on the destination and not the layover. As a mentor to many basketball players, I am frequently a sounding board when they aren't playing well or as much as they'd like.

As a big bro to athletes, I feel obligated to follow them on social media. One particular player had worked his butt off to earn a college scholarship. During the summer, before his departure to college, his Snapchat story was mundane and boring. Like clockwork, it showed how he worked out early in the morning, read the Bible, worked out again, helped his mother with his little sisters who had special needs, and hooped at night. This player had lost his father a few years earlier, and his mother was a hard-working woman who worked and took care of his sisters. His goal was to use his basketball talent to get a college education, earn a starting spot on his team, and play professionally to ease the financial burden on his mother.

His bland Snap story earned him a full ride scholarship. But when he went off to school, his Snap story went from lame to lit real quick. In the summer, he got up at 6:00 a.m. and was in bed by 10:30 p.m. Once he arrived at college, he was sleeping in until 10:00 a.m. and staying up until 3:00 a.m. His "Monday motivation" and "workout Wednesday" Snaps were replaced by "margarita Monday," "tacoooooooo Tuuuuuueeesssssdddaayyy" (Lebron voice), "wild 'n' out Wednesday," and "thirsty Thursday" Snaps. Suddenly, his Snap was poppin', but his game was lame (funny how that works).

After listening to him go on about how his coach was hatin' on him, I asked him a simple question: "Are you that same blue-collar dude who lived in the gym, or did your energy change up?" After a long sigh and a long pause, he acknowledged that he'd become caught up living the college life and had lost focus. After laughing about his Snap stories, we prayed and developed a plan of action for him to get back on track. The foundation of that plan was simple: When journeying toward your goals, don't let the layovers of life sidetrack you.

I want you to know that we all fall. The people you look up to most here on earth have lost focus before. It's essential that when you stumble, you draw closer to God and then reach out to your mentors to help you get back in your bag. Do not feel ashamed because we all have been there. But the longer you avoid getting help, the deeper you will dig yourself in and the longer it will take to dig yourself out.

And 1

- ❏ If you're not careful, your hard work will produce success that will create opportunities of temptation and distract you from your end goal.
- ❏ Have you ever lost focus on what's important as an athlete and that caused your production to slip? If so, how?
- ❏ Have you ever lost focus on what's important in your walk with God and that caused your character to slip? If so, how?
- ❏ Identify three potential distractions that could allow you to lose focus athletically and in your walk with God. Allow God and your God Squad to develop a game plan for how you can overcome the potential distractions.

Drop a Dime

- ❏ Identify at least one teammate you can hold accountable to stay focused on their athletic and spiritual goals.
- ❏ Share this message with them, and ask them if they will allow you to hold them accountable and stay focused.

PLAY THE HAND YOU'RE DEALT

SOUNDTRACK: "I GOT THAT (REMIX)" — ANTHONY BROWN & GROUP THERAPY (FEAT. 1K PHEW)

> *We are hard pressed on every side, but not crushed; perplexed, but not in despair; persecuted, but not abandoned; struck down, but not destroyed. We always carry around in our body the death of Jesus, so that the life of Jesus may also be revealed in our body.*
>
> —2 Cor. 4:8–10 NIV

We can't navigate through sports or life with a perfect hand mentality, switching teams or stacking the deck if we don't have a perfect hand. If we do, we'll miss out on an opportunity to know that, through God, we can be dealt the worst of hands and still prevail. Our focus should be to refine our God-given talents and develop a Christlike mindset that will allow us to succeed in any environment. By doing so, we place success in the hands of God instead of leaving it to chance.

We enjoy winning, but the lessons learned come from our losses. In an earlier devotional, I wrote about the ingredients needed to succeed. Sometimes taking an L is nothing more than a vital ingredient in our recipe for developing winning DNA.

Just because someone never loses doesn't mean they are a winner. Maybe they've been stacking the deck, and as a result, they win without the threat of failure. When you want to win so badly that you stack the deck, you win without developing winning DNA, and your success becomes dependent on the stacked deck. If your winning is the product of a stacked deck, what are you going to do when life turns upside down and the deck is stacked against you? You'll have no chance to win—not because you aren't capable but because you finessed the process, and it has caught up with you.

I love to play spades. Once you get dealt your hand, you can't start over and must make the most of the cards you're dealt. You'll get some winning hands and some losing ones, but you have to play it out. The same is true in life. My most fulfilling spades victories were not the times I was dealt a perfect hand but the times my hand was trash. During those instances, there were times when my partner and I felt as though we were playing against a stacked deck and nothing could go our way, but we kept playing until the tables turned and the cards began to work in our favor.

Allowing God to transform you is not easy, and there will be many days when you feel it's you against the world. Keep on trusting, and keep on fighting through God's power until the tables are turned and the blessings begin to work in your favor.

And 1

- ❑ "Your disposition should never be defined by your condition."[1]
- ❑ Sometimes, the only way to separate winners from losers is to observe how they respond to winning and losing. Describe a time when you displayed winning character in a losing circumstance, and explain the long-term benefit of your choices.

---

1. Author's notes from a sermon by Frederick Haynes III, "Can You Dig It?" February 4, 2018, Friendship-West Baptist Church, Dallas, TX.

Drop a Dime

- ❏ Ask God to reveal to you a teammate currently being dealt a losing hand. Once you establish who that is, list three positives that can come out of their being dealt that hand.
- ❏ Share with them your list, and encourage them to keep fighting until the tables turn.

BREAK THE PRESS, BEAT THE BLITZ

SOUNDTRACK: "UNSTOPPABLE" — KORYN HAWTHORNE (FEAT. YELLA BEEZY)

Finally, be strong in the Lord and in his mighty power. Put on the full armor of God, so that you can take your stand against the devil's schemes. For our struggle is not against flesh and blood, but against the rulers, against the authorities, against the powers of this dark world and against the spiritual forces of evil in the heavenly realms. Therefore put on the full armor of God, so that when the day of evil comes, you may be able to stand your ground, and after you have done everything, to stand. Stand firm then, with the belt of truth buckled around your waist, with the breastplate of righteousness in place, and with your feet fitted with the readiness that comes from the gospel of peace. In addition to all this, take up the shield of faith, with which you can extinguish all the flaming arrows of the evil one. Take the helmet of salvation and the sword of the Spirit, which is the word of God.

—Eph. 6:10–17 NIV

Great basketball teams and great players cannot be pressured. The same can be said of a good football team with a good quarterback—they cannot be blitzed. It's difficult to press a good basketball team or blitz a good football team because pressure does not bother them. A trapping or pressing defense in hoops, much like a blitz in football, is not sound because the pressure on the front end leaves holes of opportunities on the back end. They are successful and commonly used because in sports, just as in life, most fold under pressure.

When a player who lacks confidence in their ability gets pressured, they begin to make compromised decisions. Self-defeating thoughts begin to manifest internally, affecting their external performance. A composed, confident player understands that a blitz or a trap means there are holes in the defense that they can attack. They know that the defense has made themselves vulnerable down the field or down the court. If they merely trust themselves, keep their head up, and look past the pressure, there are countless opportunities for success ahead.

When coaches recognize vulnerable offenses, they turn up the heat and apply more pressure, banking on the fact that the offense will be so consumed with the pressure that they will not take advantage of the holes of opportunities ahead. On the other hand, coaches know that their "schemes" and traps will not work against composed, confident teams. Often, a team will begin to pressure another team, but when the offense attacks the pressure successfully, the coach will concede and revise the game plan. As athletes, we know the intricacies of pressure defenses, but we must also realize that the devil works in the same way. The devil knows that if we recognize who our Savior is and how powerful He is, his traps and schemes (Eph. 6:11) will not work.

Through God's power, we have the game plan to burn the blitz and break the press. Today's passage tells how to be prepared when the devil dials up the pressure. All we have to do is keep our heads up toward our target (God) and look past the pressure to the opportunities God has for us. The devil will have no choice but to concede defeat.

And 1

- ❑ As athletes, we know that a person can be equipped with all the talent and ability in the world, but if they cannot play under pressure, they will not sustain success. How does that relate to your walk with Christ and the passage from Ephesians?
- ❑ Develop three ways you can make the enemy pay for trying to pressure you into mistakes.

Drop a Dime

- ❑ Identify a teammate who needs to handle pressure better off the court. Develop a game plan with at least three ways that both of you can make the enemy pay for trying to pressure them into mistakes. Share your list for yourself, followed by your list for them.
- ❑ Ask them whether you can hold each other accountable in your quest to defeat the pressure.

LIVE THROUGH HIM

SOUNDTRACK: "KNOWN" – TAUREN WELLS

> *Saul died in disobedience, disobedient to GOD.*
> *He didn't obey GOD's words. Instead of praying, he went to a*
> *witch to seek guidance. Because he didn't go to GOD for help,*
> *GOD took his life and turned the kingdom over to*
> *David son of Jesse.*
> —1 Chron. 10:13–14 MSG

If you were the head coach of the Golden State Warriors during Jordan Bell's tenure there, would you play through Jordan—a rookie who averaged four points last season—instead of playing through Kevin Durant offensively?

Of course, you would play through KD, and with good reason. KD is arguably the best scorer on the planet. We've never seen anything like him. He's a 7-foot sniper from deep, aggressive, fantastic footwork, equipped with the shiftiness, handles, and change of direction of a guard. He's a quick jumper, 88 percent free-throw shooter, and a capable and willing passer. He can initiate offense, if needed, handle the ball on a ball screen, set the screen, and then pop and punish you.

There's nothing he can't do offensively on the court, and there's no one who can stop him from creating for himself and his teammates. Could you imagine having KD on your team and making him the fourth or fifth option on offense? In 1 Chronicles 10:13–14, God tells us how Saul died. Saul had everything going for him; he was a God-anointed king. Saul started doing his own thing instead of what God had called him to do. When Saul decided to seek the advice of fortune tellers and witches instead of God, he eventually lost his life, and David became king.

While KD is a near-perfect player, God is a never-failing, perfect God. God's will always prevails, so why would Saul choose to go his own way? It's the same reason it would make no sense to have Kevin Durant on your side and not play through him. It makes even less sense for us to have the God of the entire universe on our side and not live through Him. All Saul had to do was do what God commanded.

We have all had our fair share of Saul moments; fortunately, Jesus's blood protects us from what happened to Saul. And Saul's story provides us with a reminder that if we want to reach our potential, we must keep God as the focal point of our lives and never allow Him to be the second option.

And 1

- ❏ Identify at least one Saul moment in your journey with God and one in your athletic career, along with what happened as a result.
- ❏ What can you do to prevent Saul moments in your future walk with God and as an athlete?
- ❏ Identify at least one accountability partner who can support you as you commit to living through God in basketball and in your walk with Christ.

Drop a Dime

- ❏ Pray this prayer:

    Lord, use me. First, prepare me, then open my eyes and my heart to seek out anybody in my life who needs to commit or recommit to living through You. Lord, open up their heart to receive this devotional and use this to help us both grow closer as friends and teammates and also grow closer to You. Amen.

- ❏ If any friends or teammates come to mind, gently and lovingly share this devotional with them.

GOOD AIN'T GOOD ENOUGH

SOUNDTRACK: "CAME UP" – JOR'DAN ARMSTRONG

> *Observe people who are good at their work—skilled workers are always in demand and admired; they don't take a backseat to anyone.*
> —Prov. 22:29 MSG

I've heard that God doesn't bless mediocrity—He blesses excellence. Proverbs 22:29 states that skilled workers do not have to take a backseat to anyone. As we strive to reach our potential on the court and in our walk with God, we must understand that it's a team sport and not an individual one. Because God is omnipotent (He has unlimited power) and omnipresent (He can be everywhere at the same time), we have the Ultimate Teammate.

When I was younger, I tried to pursue success as an individual and not with my Teammate. That never ended well. While I experienced my peaks of success here and there, I was never able to remain on the mountaintop. As I matured, I humbled myself to realize I could not reach my potential on the court or in life without allowing God to lead the way.

Once I joined forces with God, I discovered that through His power, I could overcome whatever stood in my way. However, God would not unleash His divine favor if I did not do all I could. This has become my battle cry: Do all I can, and watch God do all I can't. As we prevail and reflect on our triumphs, we will conclude that, compared to God, our contribution was minimal, and God did the heavy lifting.

LeBron James has led his teams to eight straight NBA Finals. He frequently puts his teams on his back and leads them to heights only he can reach. This recipe for success is quite similar to how we should approach competing alongside our Teammate. If we are smart, we will not attempt to win on our own but will jump on God's shoulders and let Him lead us to victory.

Like LeBron's teammates, we should cultivate our strengths and trust that God will fill any void left by our weaknesses. LeBron has had many teammates with multiple vulnerabilities; in spite of that, they still play hard, and LeBron handles what they can't do. It's as if LeBron says,

> Don't worry, I know you aren't a great defender. That's okay; if your man beats you, I'll chase him down and block the shot from behind. I know you can't create off the bounce, but I am equipped to create for you. Just get to your spots of success on the floor, and I'll deliver your opportunities at just the right time. All you have to do is work on your shooting, stay ready, and I will deliver. Don't worry about what you don't have; you are on a team with the king, and what you have is more than enough.

No disrespect to LeBron and his greatness, but I am a witness to the King of all kings. God has assured me that if I cultivate my God-given strengths, I've done more than enough to win. He assures me that I need not worry about what I lack—He's got me, and together, we will overcome.

And here's the key: While God can do it all, He won't do what He gave you the ability to do. As we navigate through hoops and life, we should do so under the notion that good ain't good enough; great ain't even good enough; and 99.9 percent ain't even good enough. Only our absolute best daily is acceptable. Once we subscribe to that notion and join God's team, as Proverbs 22:29 states, we will be in high demand and never have to take a backseat to anyone.

And 1

- ❏ Be sure to read and sign the Culture Contract located at the back of this book.
- ❏ The contract states that we are committed to never allow our talent to supersede our character and that we are using our God-given talents and platforms to let God shine through us.
- ❏ As we honor the contract, we ensure that it's not us who will be in high demand but rather the God in us.

Drop a Dime

- ❏ Identify a teammate who needs to pursue excellence in God's name instead of accepting mediocrity.
- ❏ Pray for them every day for the next seven days.
- ❏ Share this devotional with them, and provide them with evidence and encouragement for why they should pursue excellence.

CULTIVATE STRENGTHS, ELIMINATE WEAKNESSES

SOUNDTRACK: "LOVE THEORY" – KIRK FRANKLIN

> *He cuts off every branch of mine that doesn't produce fruit, and he prunes the branches that do bear fruit so they will produce even more.*
> —John 15:2 NLT

As a basketball developer, when I begin to work with a new client, I have to decide what makes them unique and devise a plan to cultivate their unique talents to be even better and more consistent. I also have to determine what parts of their game they need to eliminate.

I had a client who was a knockdown shooter and one of the best spot-up shooters in college basketball. But he was undersized and lacked the athleticism to create scoring opportunities off the dribble. He insisted on playing to the things in his game that were not productive. He also was content with his ability to shoot the ball and refused to improve his gifts as a shooter. While he was a prolific shooter, he still had room to improve his range and footwork, and he needed to get his shot off more quickly.

Because he refused to continually cultivate his shooting, he fell well short of his potential as a basketball player and never reached his desired goal of playing professionally.

If the player had bought into staying away from his weaknesses and instead pruned his strengths, he would have given himself the best chance to reach his potential and fulfill his destiny. Jimmer Fredette lies on the other end of this spectrum. Over the four years we've worked together, he stays away from the areas that will not produce success and continually cultivates his strengths with humility.

Before each off-season, we discuss what he wants to improve. To my surprise, one particular off-season, his focus was to improve his shooting—specifically his range, his footwork, and getting his shot off the dribble more quickly. In spite of being one of the most prolific college basketball scorers of this generation and amassing millions of dollars, he still sought improvement.

There's a reason the college player I worked with fell short and Jimmer continues to thrive, but Jimmer was not the first or the best example of pruning and cultivating. John 15:2 is Jesus explaining to His followers God's process for Him. Jesus said that God cut off everything in Him that was not contributing to God's purpose, and the things He did that produced fruit, God pruned, allowing Jesus to produce more fruit. If we are honest with ourselves, we all have had stubborn stages where we tried to produce fruit through dead branches instead of allowing God to prune us to produce fruit in our lives. As we continue to grow in God's Word, we ought to humble ourselves and acknowledge that if Jesus, despite being perfect, was willing to be pruned, we should, too, on the court and in our journey through life for God.

And 1

- ❏ Identify a situation athletically where you were too stubborn for your own good and would not allow your coach to prune you.
- ❏ Athletically, are you currently allowing yourself to be pruned where it's needed? If so, how? If not, why not?
- ❏ In your walk with God, where does God want to cut off your dead branches?

CULTIVATE STRENGTHS, ELIMINATE WEAKNESSES

- ❏ Identify a time when God cut off branches that were not producing fruit, and identify the fruit that was produced.

Drop a Dime
- ❏ Identify at least one teammate who needs to allow God to cut off their dead branches and be pruned.
- ❏ Share this devotional with them, and share with them where you have been pruned and where you are struggling to allow God to cut off dead branches.
- ❏ Ask them to pray for you.
- ❏ Ask them where they need to have branches cut off and where they need to allow God to prune them, and ask if they will let you hold them accountable.

PUT THE BALL IN GOD'S HANDS

SOUNDTRACK: "SO MUCH LUV" – JOR'DAN ARMSTRONG

> *And we know that God causes everything to work together for the good of those who love God and are called according to his purpose for them.*
> —Rom. 8:28 NLT

While many have identified Tom Brady as the G.O.A.T. (Greatest of All Time), I'm more of an Aaron Rogers guy. I think that if Rogers and Brady had switched teams, Rogers would have been just as successful after spending his entire career with the Patriots organization and head coach Bill Belichick. But that's another debate for another day.

What's not up for debate is that when the ball is in the hands of Aaron Rogers, the Green Bay Packers' chance of victory significantly increases. As you might imagine, when backup running back and kick returner Ty Montgomery decided to run the ball out of the end zone on a kickoff, many in the organization were upset. With just over two minutes remaining in the game, the Packers trailed the league's best team, the Los Angeles Rams, by only two points. And reportedly, Montgomery was instructed to down the kickoff in the end zone to maximize the time the ball would be in Rogers's hand.

Unfortunately for Montgomery, Rogers, and the other Packers, his decision to run the ball out of the end zone instead of downing it backfired when he fumbled the ball and the Rams took over, running out the clock. With that loss, the Packers' chances of making the playoffs decreased significantly. Montgomery's teammates voiced their frustration in postgame interviews, explaining that they had one of the best quarterbacks in the history of the game who had just led them to a miraculous, come-from-behind win the game before. They had complete faith that, if given the ball, Rogers would have done it again.

The intent of this devotional is not to kick Montgomery while he's down—he's an accomplished NFL player, and one mistake does not define him just as one mistake does not define us. I am, however, using his unfortunate blunder to bring to light that we, too, have sometimes mistakenly kept possession and tried to make the heroic play ourselves instead of putting our lives in God's hands and allowing Him to lead us to yet another come-from-behind victory.

Like Montgomery, we have to learn from our previous mistakes and ensure moving forward that God has possession. God and great quarterbacks have a common characteristic: The longer they possess the ball, the less likely the opposition will prevail. In football and in life, the enemy will do whatever he can to keep the ball out of the hands of a great quarterback. Moving forward, we should live life with the same mindset of the defense of a great quarterback. All we have to do is get the ball in the hands of our Quarterback. He's never failed and has brought us from behind time and time again. In fact, God promises He will cause everything to work together for our victory, as stated in Romans 8:28. All we have to do is put the ball in His hands.

As you meditate on this devotional and look to apply it to your life and career, take note of a few of Cherie Carter-Scott's rules for being human:

- *You will learn lessons.*
- *There are no mistakes, only lessons.*

- *A lesson is repeated until learned.*
- *Learning lessons does not end.*

And 1

- ❑ In what areas of your life do you need to place the ball in God's hands?
- ❑ List previous moments in which you kept the ball and as a result took an L instead of allowing God to take control.
- ❑ After reviewing the rules for being human, ask God to reveal to you what lessons you need to learn so you will not continue to make the same mistakes. Once identified, list them in your journal, and continually pray for God to lead you to learn from previous mistakes.

Drop a Dime

- ❑ Share this devotional with a teammate, and challenge one another to put your life and career in God's hands and learn from all your previous mistakes.

GROWING PAINS

SOUNDTRACK: "PAIN" – 1K PHEW

There's more to come: We continue to shout our praise even when we're hemmed in with troubles, because we know how troubles can develop passionate patience in us, and how that patience in turn forges the tempered steel of virtue, keeping us alert for whatever God will do next. In alert expectancy such as this, we're never left feeling shortchanged. Quite the contrary—we can't round up enough containers to hold everything God generously pours into our lives through the Holy Spirit!

—Rom. 5:3–5 MSG

As a seventh-grade boy, I lived the above verses from Romans. One day in the summer, I woke up excited to feel my knees hurting. To those who never desired to play basketball at a high level, this may not make much sense, but for the real hoopers, you understand the joy that comes when you have Osgood-Schlatter. It's the pain that occurs before and during growth spurts.

Aspiring basketball players understand that the taller they are, the better chance they have to reach their goals in basketball. Currently, I am a little bit south of 6 feet and considered below average height for a basketball player. When I was 12, I was extremely short for my age. I knew that for my basketball dreams to become a reality, I would need significant growth spurts.

As we journey through our athletic careers and, more importantly, through life and our walk with Christ, we should have my mindset at the age of 12; when we feel growing pains, it's time to rejoice instead of feeling discouraged. While we may not see the growth yet, God can produce the growth spurt needed for us to reach our goals in athletics and in our Christian lives.

Minus the proper perspective, we will assume the pains we are going through are walls that will prevent us from reaching our destiny. Instead, it could be that God has heard every one of the big dreams we prayed to Him and has diagnosed us with a spiritual case of Osgood-Schlatter to generate a growth spurt.

The late, great Nelson Mandela said it best: "Difficulties break some men but make others. No axe is sharp enough to cut the soul of a sinner who keeps on trying, one armed with the hope that he will rise even in the end."[1] In Jesus's name, keep on going; keep on growing.

And 1

- ❑ Reflect on a time on the court when you went through a painful period that allowed you to grow into a better player.
- ❑ Now, do the same off the court. Reflect on a time when a painful period produced spiritual growth.

---

1. "Selected Quotes," *Nelson Mandela Foundation*, https://www.nelsonmandela.org/content/page/selected-quotes.

Drop a Dime

- ❏ Identify a teammate currently going through a period of pain who does not realize that this pain will produce a much-needed growth spurt. Reach out to them, and encourage them to keep going and keep growing.

BE AGGRESSIVE OR LOSE THE LEAD

SOUNDTRACK: "PUT ME IN COACH" – DEE-1

> *But thanks be to God, who gives us the victory through our Lord Jesus Christ.*
> —1 Cor. 15:57 ESV

When you're on top, you are vulnerable to losing your lead both in life and in basketball if you stop being aggressive. In athletics, we have all played in a game when our team came out aggressive, fueling them to play confidently, take command of the game, and sprint to a substantial, double-digit lead. But at some point during the game, they lost aggression and stopped attacking, and the large seemingly insurmountable lead rapidly began to shrink. The more the lead dwindled, the less secure the team felt, and they eventually blew the lead.

After such a game, the team is in the dark, somber locker room trying to make sense of how they lost such a big lead. The reason they'd built such a huge lead was that they'd come out expecting victory. But once they got the lead and the opposition made an aggressive run at them, they got uptight, and their once-fearless mindset was replaced by a cautious disposition.

In basketball, good teams and good players are able to play with a lead because they stay in attack mode. They are able to turn a 10-point lead into a 30-point blowout. The same can be said for us in our walk with Christ. Just as our coaches want us to do in hoops, God wants us to do in life, to win instead of just living not to lose. In fact, through Jesus's victory of overcoming death for us, we can do even better than live to win—we can live with a we've-already-won mentality because through Him, we already have. That's right! Victory for us has already been secured. No matter how bad our situation may appear, all we have to do is show up, compete, and expect the W.

In life, it's no different than in basketball. You can lose a game and still be a champion. When a championship-caliber team loses a game, they merely watch film to identify the root of the loss, address it, and move on—and we can do the same in our life's journey. We've all lost a lead in life because we allowed life's aggressiveness to prevent us from living in attack mode. All we have to do is watch film with our Coach and let Him make adjustments while trusting that no matter how many games we lose, we'll still be part of God's championship team.

And 1

- ❏ Reflect back to a game in sports when you lost the lead because you stopped attacking. Take yourself back to the locker room after the game, and rekindle those feelings of frustration you had, knowing you should have won.
- ❏ Relate that to a period in your life outside basketball when you stopped being aggressive, and compare the similarities.
- ❏ Are you afraid of living life in attack mode for Christ? If so, what can you do to overcome that fear?

Drop a Dime

- ❏ Identify a teammate who is falling short of their potential on the court and in life because they are afraid to live and play aggressively.
- ❏ Share this devotional with them, and express to them what gifts, talents, and characteristics God has gifted them with to allow them to be more aggressive.

UNSEEN HOURS

SOUNDTRACK: "DREAMIN'" — JUSTIN MATTHEW

*"Master," said David, "don't give up hope.
I'm ready to go and fight this Philistine."*

*Saul answered David, "You can't go and fight this Philistine.
You're too young and inexperienced—and he's been at this
fighting business since before you were born."*

*David said, "I've been a shepherd, tending sheep for my father.
Whenever a lion or bear came and took a lamb from the flock,
I'd go after it, knock it down, and rescue the lamb. If it turned
on me, I'd grab it by the throat, wring its neck, and kill it.
Lion or bear, it made no difference—I killed it. And I'll do the
same to this Philistine pig who is taunting the troops of God-
Alive. GOD, who delivered me from the teeth of the lion and the
claws of the bear, will deliver me from this Philistine."*

Saul said, "Go. And GOD help you!"
—1 Sam. 17:32–37 MSG

We've all heard the story of David defeating Goliath. Without question, it's the biggest upset in the history of humankind. It's such a mind-blowing story that we tend to overlook David's commitment to preparation. Have you ever wondered what David did to prepare for victory? If we aren't careful, we can assume that while David displayed great courage, maybe it was just his lucky day or he prevailed because he caught Goliath by surprise.

But David's victory was birthed out of obedience to what God called him to do daily. David's commitment to preparation provides us with a blueprint, and if we follow suit, we, too, will slay our upcoming Goliath-like battles in basketball and in life. As we navigate through our athletic careers, we should adopt a W.W.D.D. approach: What Would David Do?

We've all heard this saying: Character is what you do when no one is watching. In basketball, we know that the unseen hours will show up when the lights come on. During David's unseen hours, he was protecting the sheep by killing lions and bears. Could you imagine having such commitment to your job that you would kill a lion?

While David was routinely killing lions and bears, he wasn't getting any love or acknowledgment, but despite the lack of public recognition, he didn't stop slaying lions. His brothers looked the part and were regarded as the ones who were next up, and everybody looked down at David as the little shepherd boy.

Because of David's rigorous daily routine of killing lions, fighting Goliath was light work. When Goliath pulled up, our boy David was ready to kick butt and take names. Everybody else ran and hid, but David stepped up, prepared to slay the giant. While the results were a surprise to everyone else, David was not surprised because he was prepared in private.

Here are the takeaways for us:
- What would have happened if David hadn't dominated his unseen hours? Obviously, Goliath would have had his way with him, and David's people would have paid the price.
- If David hadn't obeyed God and willingly done what he was called to do, he would not have developed his skills. As an athlete, you

may be on the scout team or JV, but if you ask yourself what David would do, you will take pride in your work and trust that the lions you are facing in private will prepare you to prevail against the Goliaths in public.
- To prepare for the season, we should follow David's lead and look to defeat lions and bears even during the off-season.

And 1

- ❏ Keep it 100 with yourself. Are you defeating lions and bears in order to prevail against your Goliaths on the court and in everyday life? If so, list them. If not, list the lions and bears that you are avoiding.
- ❏ Identify a time when you didn't take David's approach to your unseen hours, complaining and doing the job halfheartedly instead of taking pride in your work. What were the results?
- ❏ Identify a situation in your life right now where you need to change your perspective, and instead ask yourself: What Would David Do (W.W.D.D.)?

Drop a Dime

- ❏ Encourage at least one teammate who needs to realize that God has put them in a situation that may not be fun right now but is going to allow them to develop fruit in the future. Share with them David's story of preparation.
- ❏ Commit to preparing yourself to dominate your unseen hours like David so you can be an inspiration to a teammate, just as David is to you.

WHERE MY REAL FRIENDS AT?

SOUNDTRACK: "FRIENDS" – ANDY MINEO

A friend is always loyal, and a brother is born to help in time of need.
—Prov. 17:17 NLT

Friends love through all kinds of weather, and families stick together in all kinds of trouble.
—Prov. 17:17 MSG

Everyone in your camp ain't necessarily in your corner. Just because you're teammates with others does not mean you are friends or as close as family. In sports, we loosely refer to our teammates as our brothers and sisters, but when it's time to put those words into action, we often fall short. As followers of Christ, we should strive to be both friends and brothers or sisters to those on our team. We can use Proverbs 17:17 to audit whether we are truly supporting our teammates. Let's dig deeper!

Are we friends to those on our team?

I know we say we are, and we have probably convinced ourselves that we are, but the proof is in the pudding. If we are, we must examine whether we have been loyal to our teammates during their toughest times.

Are we true brothers or sisters to our teammates?

If we are, then we prove our support during their times of need, not just in their times of glory. It's great to celebrate with our teammates when they are riding waves of success; however, brothers and sisters are there when the ball is not bouncing their way.

Often, those who are overlooked and dismissed are the very ones who need us the most. It's easy to go out with the teammate who just had a 30 piece, develop a friendship with the all-American, or keep in touch with the teammate who just got drafted into the NBA or WNBA. There's nothing wrong with that, but not at the expense of lifting up your teammate who went from starting to not getting in the game, or befriending the walk-on that many overlook, or staying in touch with the player who didn't make it professionally.

We should make sure no one on our team will ever have to go through trying times without the love and support of real friends and teammates. In fact, I'd venture to say there's someone in your locker room right now who's hurting and in need of a true friend. If you're a former player, I'm sure one of your former teammates is going through something and needs a brother or a sister.

You never know that God is all you need until He's all you have. As this relates to our teams, your teammates will never know that Christ-led teammates are what they need until that's all they have. I've heard that 25 percent of the people in your life don't like you and never will; 25 percent don't like you unless you're trending up and they'll rock with you; 25 percent like you until you get knocked down; and 25 percent will ride or die for you no matter what. We don't ever want our teammates to fail, but when your teammates hit their valleys in life and in hoops, that's when they need you to prove you are, indeed, their friend and a brother or sister who will ride or die with them until the wheels fall off.

And 1

- ☐ Ask God to reveal to you how you can be a better teammate.
- ☐ Ask God to reveal to you who on your team needs you to be a better teammate.

Drop a Dime

- ☐ Based on what God revealed, develop a plan of action to be a true friend and as close as a brother or sister to all your teammates. Implement the plan immediately.
- ☐ Share this devotional with the leaders or captains of your team. If you are a leader or captain, share it with your fellow leaders and collectively develop a plan of action to create a culture of great teammates.

HOLD ONTO YOUR HOW

SOUNDTRACK: "DROWN" – LECRAE (FEAT. JOHN LEGEND)

It was reported to David that the Philistines were raiding Keilah and looting the grain. David went in prayer to GOD: "Should I go after these Philistines and teach them a lesson?"

GOD said, "Go. Attack the Philistines and save Keilah."

But David's men said, "We live in fear of our lives right here in Judah. How can you think of going to Keilah in the thick of the Philistines?"

So David went back to GOD in prayer. GOD said, "Get going. Head for Keilah. I'm placing the Philistines in your hands."

—1 Sam. 23:1–4 MSG

Immature Christians and immature athletes are similar—both are susceptible to changing once they taste success. The devil is out to steal, kill, and destroy us, and one of his most successful methods is using success. If we aren't careful, the devil will finesse us into letting go of our how. Once we do, we will abandon the process of success and begin to arrogantly navigate through life and athletics independently instead of remaining humble and allowing God and those He has placed in our lives to lead us.

We must never forget that we win because God prepares and leads us. While He leads, He also goes ahead of us to develop our future. As players, that means God equipped the player development coach to devise a development plan, He touched an assistant coach to enhance our IQ every Wednesday in film sessions, He anointed the strength coach to create a stretch and recovery plan every Monday, and He prepared the head coach to identify how we could thrive in the offense. All that preparation allowed us to be selected as the conference player of the week, to earn a starting spot, or to get drafted.

As a child of God, have you identified your how? As a player, have you recognized your how? If you have yet to discover your how, figure it out. If you have, never let go of it, because that's your blueprint to replicate the success you've experienced.

David was on the fast track to becoming king. He pulled off the greatest upset when he slayed Goliath with a few stones and a slingshot. If anyone had the right to not seek guidance and instead trust themselves and their own instincts, it would have been David at this particular moment. Instead, David provided a blueprint for us as leaders in life and on the court.

1. He did not allow his success to blind him to how he'd previously succeeded. He knew it was God's guidance and continued to urgently seek Him in moments of distress, just as he did when he beat Goliath.
2. He did not let the perceived urgency of the situation speed him into making a decision without being led by God. Even in the moment of distress, he stopped to pray and ask God for guidance.

There are two types of people in life: those who are humbled and those who are about to be. The way I see it, through God's leadership, we can remain humble and allow Him to guide us to repeated victories in our walk with Him. On the court, we can stay mindful of the coaches and support staff who make significant contributions to our success and remain coachable as we level up. Or we can lose sight of our how and, in turn, lose everything we have worked so hard for.

And 1

- ❏ Identify how you can respond to success like David did, both in your spiritual walk and in sports.

Drop a Dime

- ❏ Share this devotional with one of your teammates who is currently on a successful wave. Gently push them to handle success like David.

LOSE YOUR HOW, LOSE YOUR SPOT (PART I)

SOUNDTRACK: "REAL" – ANTHONY BROWN & GROUP THERAPY (FEAT. JONATHAN MCREYNOLDS)

> *But Samuel replied, "What is more pleasing to the LORD: your burnt offerings and sacrifice or your obedience to his voice? Listen! Obedience is better than sacrifice, and submission is better than offering the fat of rams. Rebellion is as sinful as witchcraft, and stubbornness as bad as worshiping idols. So because you have rejected the command of the LORD, he has rejected you as king."*
>
> *Then Saul admitted to Samuel, "Yes, I have sinned. I have disobeyed your instructions and the LORD's command, for I was afraid of the people and did what they demanded."*
>
> 1 Sam. 15:22–24 NLT

> *When Saul saw the vast Philistine army, he became frantic with fear. He asked the LORD what he should do, but the LORD refused to answer him, either by dreams or by sacred lots or by the prophets.*
>
> —1 Sam. 28:5–6 NLT

As mentioned in the previous devotional, if we are not careful, the devil will manipulate us into letting go of our how. Ignoring our how will likely lead to forgetting Who has allowed us to overcome, which leads to self-centeredness, a lack of humility, and a reliance on self instead of complete dependence on God.

En route to becoming king, David frequently experienced victory because he remained mindful that God was the source of His success. His mindfulness of what God did for him kept him humble and dependent on God. On the other hand, Saul, whom David replaced as king, forgot his how, did not allow God to lead him every step of the way, and eventually disobeyed God's direction for him as a leader.

Saul's disobedience and reliance on self are what led him to lose his kingship and eventually his life. All Saul had to do was let God take control, and he would have remained king. As athletes, we must recognize those people God placed in our lives to guide us toward sustained success. As we realize who those people are, we have a choice. Are we going to follow David's example or Saul's? Are we going to remain humble and coachable to those whose guidance produced a profit on the court and in our character development, or are we going to reject encouraging leadership as Saul did?

After reading the previous devotional, we should all have identified our how on and off the court. The ball is in our court to stay committed to our how by remaining committed to God's gentle guidance and leadership. We should continue to be led by the people God has anointed to guide us, pursuing our godly destinies as leaders for Christ in our communities and in basketball. Just as David provided us with our blueprint for success, Saul's cautionary tale offers a reminder of what will likely happen if we reject God's leadership.

1. Leaders who lack obedience to God and the godly people placed in their lives will face defeat.
2. If you forget your how long enough and instead choose to do life your way, God may not answer when you get in over your head.

As athletes, we will not lose our lives for rejecting leadership, but if we choose to navigate through our playing careers as Saul did instead of as

LOSE YOUR HOW, LOSE YOUR SPOT (PART I)

David did, we will likely have similar results. Saul lost his spot to David, not because Saul was incapable of being king but because Saul refused to be coachable. It's unfortunate to read about Saul losing such a coveted position because of his foolish pride and ego, but it would also be sad for us to lose our coveted spots in basketball and in our walk with Christ because of pride.

And 1

- ❏ Identify at least one Saul moment in sports that you've had, along with the result.

Drop a Dime

- ❏ Ask God to put on your heart which member of your team needs to convert from a Saul mindset to a David mindset.
- ❏ Once you identify who it is, stay in continued prayer, and with your actions, influence them to transition to a David mindset.

LOSE YOUR HOW, LOSE YOUR SPOT (PART II)

SOUNDTRACK: "NO GRAY" — JONATHAN MCREYNOLDS

*One late afternoon, David got up from taking his nap
and was strolling on the roof of the palace.
From his vantage point on the roof he saw a woman bathing.
The woman was stunningly beautiful.
David sent to ask about her, and was told,
"Isn't this Bathsheba, daughter of Eliam and
wife of Uriah the Hittite?" David sent his agents to get her.
After she arrived, he went to bed with her.
(This occurred during the time of "purification"
following her period.) Then she returned home.
Before long she realized she was pregnant.*

Later she sent word to David: "I'm pregnant."

. . .

*In the morning David wrote a letter to Joab and sent it with
Uriah. In the letter he wrote, "Put Uriah in the front lines where
the fighting is the fiercest. Then pull back and leave him exposed
so that he's sure to be killed."*

—2 Sam. 11:2–5, 14–15 MSG

> *You murdered Uriah the Hittite, then took his wife as your wife. Worse, you killed him with an Ammonite sword! And now, because you treated God with such contempt and took Uriah the Hittite's wife as your wife, killing and murder will continually plague your family. This is GOD speaking, remember! I'll make trouble for you out of your own family. I'll take your wives from right out in front of you. I'll give them to some neighbor, and he'll go to bed with them openly. You did your deed in secret; I'm doing mine with the whole country watching!"*
>
> *Then David confessed to Nathan,
> "I've sinned against GOD."*
>
> *Nathan pronounced, "Yes, but that's not the last word.
> GOD forgives your sin. You won't die for it.
> But because of your blasphemous behavior,
> the son born to you will die."*
>
> —2 Sam. 12:9–14 MSG

If you read through 1 Samuel and the first 10 chapters of 2 Samuel, or if you have read many of the devotionals in this book, you probably have grown to respect and admire the character of David. Throughout his journey from being an overlooked shepherd boy to God's anointed king, David remained humble and maintained a willingness to be led by God.

To paraphrase 2 Samuel 11, David noticed Bathsheba, a beautiful woman, bathing. David was told she was married, yet he still pursued an immoral, intimate relationship with her, causing Bathsheba to become pregnant. David then devised a plan for her husband to die by placing him on the front line of the battlefield.

The same David who has provided us with an example of what it means to trust in and follow God has now impregnated a married woman and arranged for the execution of her husband. That should remind us that minus God's presence and guidance, even the most righteous people are capable of immoral actions.

LOSE YOUR HOW, LOSE YOUR SPOT (PART II)

As we examine David's bad decision, we should not look down on David because we have all been there in one way or another. Instead, we should attempt to do what David did not: learn from Saul's mistake. Keep in mind that David witnessed the crumbling of Saul's kingdom because of Saul's pride and ego—despite that, David still made this colossal mistake.

In basketball and every other area of life, if we remain humble and obedient to God, we will reach mountaintops. To stay there, we must remember the following:

1. Never forget it's God's Spirit and guidance that produce the character and integrity needed to be a leader—be it a king, a queen, a team captain, a senior leader, a leader of a youth group, a coach, or a parent. We must remain humble and realize that minus God's spirit and guidance, we are capable of doing evil and disobedient acts that affect not only us but many close to us. Both Saul and David lost their sons because of their godless actions. As athletes, our teammates will probably not lose their lives; however, our actions could impact both the quality and longevity of their playing careers.
2. One of the devil's biggest weapons is distraction. David was caught off guard and distracted by Bathsheba. The devil's ability to shift David's focus to the wrong thing led to David's making bad decisions with negative consequences. We must stay on guard and focus on God so the devil can't distract us from our destiny as athletes and leaders for God.

As a result of one awful decision, so much of what David had worked so hard for was compromised. Throughout David's journey, he had successfully won battles in God's name because of his unwavering obedience. God blessed David with everything he needed and also provided him with His protection. I hope we will all pursue athletics like David pursued becoming king. If we do, we, too, will receive God's favor and protection. My prayer is that, unlike David, we will be prepared for the devil's distractions. After all, God did not bring us this far just to lose it all. He has more success for us in every aspect of our lives, not just basketball.

And 1

- ❑ Remember, minus God's presence and guidance, we are all capable of immoral actions that could jeopardize our success and the well-being of others. Take five to 10 minutes in prayer and consider what you could compromise athletically and in every other area of your life if you lose focus like David did.

Drop a Dime

- ❑ Continue to allow God to transform you into a person who keeps God first as you allow God to use you to influence your teammates to do the same.

ROCK SOLID

SOUNDTRACK: "THE NARROW ROAD" — DEE-1 (FEAT. CHRISTON GRAY)

"So everyone who hears these words of Mine and acts on them, will be like a wise man [a far-sighted, practical, and sensible man] who built his house on the rock. And the rain fell, and the floods and torrents came, and the winds blew and slammed against that house; yet it did not fall, because it had been founded on the rock. And everyone who hears these words of Mine and does not do them, will be like a foolish (stupid) man who built his house on the sand. And the rain fell, and the floods and torrents came, and the winds blew and slammed against that house; and it fell—and great and complete was its fall."

When Jesus had finished [speaking] these words [on the mountain], the crowds were astonished and overwhelmed at His teaching.

—Matt. 7:24–28 AMP

Jesus's profound words in the above verses are words to live by, both in our walk with Him and our athletic journeys. During the off-season, players have a choice: They can build their game on rock or on sand. They can choose to get through the workout, or they can select the uncommon approach and squeeze every ounce of potential out of the workout.

The difference between those who build their game on rock versus those who build on sand is not revealed in the off-season, and it may not even show up early in the season. I was fortunate to spend the 2017–2018 season as a staff member at Iowa State. We played in the toughest conference in the country that season—the Big 12. Every night was a dogfight, and every night we faced NBA-caliber talent and Hall-of-Fame-level coaching. If we were on the road, we had an entire community against us—hotel maids, restaurant servers, bus drivers, referees, and, of course, thousands of fans at the game.

During our non-conference schedule, players who had built their game on sand may have been able to get by, but once January rolled around and we entered conference play, their foundation was exposed. As it states in the verses from Matthew, they not only failed but they failed hard and often. On the other hand, the players who took no shortcuts in the off-season experienced the same harsh challenges but were able to persevere.

Once conference play started, we were faced with fierce competition twice a week for 10 straight weeks. It was all gas and no brakes as the challenges came at us fast and hard. There were a few players who attempted to build their houses on rock in January, but it was too late for them to break down their current game and build it stronger. Had they heeded the advice of coaches and older players, they would have been able to withstand the storm.

In our walk with God, we will experience challenging times. If we choose to weasel our way through rough stretches of life instead of using those challenges to develop our character, we will not be equipped to prevail in the future. Much like a player trying to build their game in the middle of the season, we, too, will have no chance to overcome. After all, you can't build a house to withstand a storm during the actual storm—that's a commitment that must be made long before the storm is on the horizon.

And 1
- ☐ Spiritually, what are you doing to build your faith on a firm foundation?
- ☐ Athletically, what are you doing to develop your game on a strong foundation?

Drop a Dime
- ☐ Assist at least one teammate in building a strong foundation in their walk with God and their game.

KNOW-IT-ALLS ALWAYS FAIL

SOUNDTRACK: "FOLLOW THE DRIP" – DAVIES

> *Trust in the LORD with all your heart; do not depend on your own understanding. Seek his will in all you do, and he will show you which path to take. Don't be impressed with your own wisdom. Instead, fear the LORD and turn away from evil. Then you will have healing for your body and strength for your bones.*
> —Prov. 3:5–8 NLT

> *Trust GOD from the bottom of your heart; don't try to figure out everything on your own. Listen for GOD's voice in everything you do, everywhere you go; he's the one who will keep you on track. Don't assume that you know it all. Run to GOD! Run from evil! Your body will glow with health, your very bones will vibrate with life!*
> —Prov. 3:5–8 MSG

A few years ago, one of the players I mentor (let's call him Jervae) was preparing for his freshman season. Because he had never played at that level, he did not know what to expect. As a result, he relied on my wisdom and knowledge and on many others who played at a high level. His decision to embrace the guidance of others who had his best interests at heart paid huge dividends as he thrived during his freshman season.

But Jervae underperformed his sophomore season. When he came to train the summer before his sophomore year, he did not embrace the wisdom of older players and coaches nearly as much as he had before his freshman year. His success convinced him that he had it all figured out and that he was at a place athletically to depend on his own understanding (Prov. 3). Most of us can relate—we've been in that arrogant space where our success made us feel like we had it figured out. We don't watch film like we used to, we halfheartedly listen to coaches' instructions, and we go through the motions during weights and agilities. We don't recognize the slippage until the underclassmen take our spot, the lesser talented yet determined team smacks us at home, or our coach calls us into the office and tells us our scholarship is not being renewed. Then we look back, and our blind spots become visible. We have to live with the fact that our decrease in production is our own fault, and we think to ourselves, "How did this happen? How did I lose myself? I used to be the first one to get to the gym and the last one to leave, and now I'm one of the last to arrive and the first to leave."

When we allow success to convince us that we have everything figured out, we lose our urgency, and our once-urgent disposition is slowly replaced with complacency. I've concluded that I should navigate through sports and my walk with Christ with an I'm-in-over-my-head mindset. That's when I'm at my best. When I was a freshman, I listened intently to my coaches and older teammates, which is why I was prepared for success. When I got older, there were times that I assumed I knew it all, but every time I felt like I knew it all, I began to fail. As I have matured in my walk with Christ, I have finally come to the conclusion that I will never have it figured out and that God is always up to something in my life. He is always preparing me to level up, and what was good enough for my current success in basketball and life is not good enough for where He wants to take me.

The verses above from Proverbs state that we should trust in the Lord with all our heart and never assume we have it figured out. Notice that it does not say to trust in the Lord until you have a 20-point game and then rely on your own understanding. It does not say you can trust in the Lord with all your heart when you are young and inexperienced, but once you've gone to Bible study for a few years, you can rely on your own understanding. It says that no matter how much you achieve, you can't rely on your own knowledge but should always run to God's Word.

Here are some major keys to sustaining success and continuing to level up:

1. Without God's presence, we will settle for significantly less than what God is calling us to do in sports and in our overall life's journey.
2. God's plan is too much for us to handle all at once, so He provides us with just the right amount of knowledge, wisdom, and experience for the task at hand. If He gave us more than that, we'd be overwhelmed. While He provides us with just enough to prevail at the level we are currently in, that won't be enough for what He has next. Our thinking is flawed if we assume we can succeed at the next level of athletics or life with the knowledge and wisdom He's provided at the current stage.
3. We are so much better when we realize we can't make it on our own but, instead, must depend on God and the godly people in our lives for knowledge and guidance.
4. We should never strive to be know-it-alls. Instead, we should push to learn as much as we can, understanding we will never learn it all. But as we humbly and urgently pursue learning as much as we can while relying on God's wisdom, we will always be prepared to move when God is ready to level us up.

And 1
- ❏ Start a journal if you haven't already. In your journal, write down the major keys from this devotional, and refer to them frequently to keep you grounded during success.

Drop a Dime
- ❏ Share your major keys with one of your teammates.

MAKE IT RAIN (LIKE ELIJAH)

SOUNDTRACK: "GOD'S GOT A BLESSING" – NORMAN HUTCHINS

> *Make this your common practice: Confess your sins to each other and pray for each other so that you can live together whole and healed. The prayer of a person living right with God is something powerful to be reckoned with. Elijah, for instance, human just like us, prayed hard that it wouldn't rain, and it didn't—not a drop for three and a half years. Then he prayed that it would rain, and it did. The showers came and everything started growing again.*
> —James 5:16–18 MSG

In the God Swag devotional, we discussed the swag Elijah had because of his connection to God. Elijah's motives were for God's purposes to be carried out and to help God's people. That notion is echoed here in the verses from James, which state that Elijah was a righteous person who leveraged his righteousness not for personal gain but for the betterment of his teammates.

If we genuinely care about our teammates, coaches, friends, family, and community, then these passages should provide us with the incentive to pursue righteous living. They should also ignite our souls to be more obedient, allowing us to become more righteous each day. As a result, our prayers for our teammates, on the court and in life, will be much more powerful and effective, just as they were for Elijah, one of our role models. If we genuinely want the best for our teammates, the most loving thing we can do for them is to not shout them out on IG, to send them an encouraging text when times are tough, and to treat them to lunch. While those heartfelt deeds are admirable, the most loving thing we can do is be obedient and pray for them just like the big homie, Elijah.

As you read this book, I hope it leads you to further invest in your personal relationship with God. I am convinced that once you have done so, you will grow in obedience and become more righteous. My challenge for all of us is that our motivation for righteousness is not just about how it will benefit us but, instead, how we can allow God to work through us to positively impact our teams on and off the court.

There is supernatural power in the prayers of those who are living right for God. Like any good superhero (we may not be a superhero, but when we are righteous, our Superhero works through us), use your power selflessly for the good of those around you. Imagine how powerful a team of players with an Elijah-like spirit could be?

And 1

- ❏ Think about what you think about. As you grow in Christ, intentionally visualize how your powerful prayers will affect those around you.

Drop a Dime

- ❏ Put this into action. Pray like Elijah for your teammates. Remember, by drawing closer to God and allowing Him to lead, you are more righteous today than you were yesterday, so your prayers have more power.

INTERNAL DRIVE LEADS TO EXTERNAL SUCCESS

SOUNDTRACK: "YES YOU CAN" – MARVIN SAPP

> *Preach the word of God. Be prepared,*
> *whether the time is favorable or not. Patiently correct,*
> *rebuke, and encourage your people with good teaching.*
> —2 Tim. 4:2 NLT

For the most part, athletes fall into one of three categories. The first are players who only become urgent about their game when crap hits the fan. They lose their starting spot or get cut, get embarrassed on national TV, or are in the midst of an extreme shooting slump. Once they feel they have hit rock bottom, they subscribe to the process needed to thrive athletically. But as soon as these players feel they are back on top, they again lose urgency and remain on a roller-coaster ride between excellence and self-inflicted disaster.

Second are players who remain urgent and committed to their craft as long as things are going well externally. If the coaches are gassing them up, they go hard in practice; if they are trending on Twitter, they grind;

and if they have a five-game stretch averaging 23 points, they're gym rats. However, when their yang turns to yen, category two athletes act totally different. When their coach changes up and goes from praising them to punishing them, their effort evaporates. When they get trolled on social media for their inconsistent play, they lose commitment to the grind; and when they go from averaging 23 points to barely playing, they're no longer gym rats. These players' dependence on external success to drive internal commitment will produce the same roller-coaster ride as players in the first category. And when they hit a rough patch, they'll fall deeper into their valleys and lack the internal drive to change course.

Very few players are in the third category. Think Tom Brady or the late Kobe Bryant. The third type of player wakes up every day with a commitment and urgency to be the best player possible. It's their internal maturity that allows them to not be influenced by external circumstances. At 40 years old, Tom Brady has the same urgency he did as a 22-year-old rookie, if not more. The same was true for Kobe—he was just as driven to win his fifth title as he was to win his first one. When things aren't going well, players in this category still have an urgent work ethic. When they're winning MVPs and championships, that same energy remains, and they still urgently subscribe to the same process of greatness.

We need to take time and reflect on what type of Christian we are. Today's verse is challenging us to be the same type of Christians as the category 3 athletes described above. We must refuse to be the type of Christian who spends time with God only when something catastrophic happens such as losing our job, getting ill, or falling behind financially. When God bails us out, we bail on Him. We can't be spiritually weak either, losing faith in God when things get tough and getting discouraged to the point where a small speed bump develops into a huge roadblock.

The only way we will reach God's greatness here on earth is if we wake up every day to practice urgency in our relationship with God, despite what's occurring externally. Urgently praise, worship, and seek God when you feel like you are on top of the world, down in the dumps, or anywhere in between. As you do, even the careers of Tom Brady and Kobe Bryant will pale in comparison to the greatness God has in store for you.

And 1

- ❑ Commit to urgently follow God with faith and expectancy through life's ups and downs.
- ❑ Through God's power, commit to urgently working on your game with faith and expectancy through the ups and downs.

Drop a Dime

- ❑ Share this devotional with at least one teammate, encouraging them to approach their faith and sports as Brady and Bryant approached athletics.

STOP SETTLING: BAD SHOTS WILL GET YOU BEAT ON AND OFF THE COURT

SOUNDTRACK: "BLESSINGS" — LECRAE (FEAT. TY DOLLA SIGN)

*Yet what we suffer now is nothing compared to
the glory he will reveal to us later.*
—Rom. 8:18 NLT

*May you experience the love of Christ, though it is too great to
understand fully. Then you will be made complete with all the
fullness of life and power that comes from God.
Now all glory to God, who is able, through his mighty
power at work within us, to accomplish infinitely more than
we might ask or think.*
—Eph. 3:19–20 NLT

*That He would grant you, according to the riches of
His glory, to be strengthened with might through
His Spirit in the inner man.*
—Eph. 3:16 NKJV

Like any great coach, God hates to see His players settle. As players, we've all taken a bad shot, and as we glance over at our coach, we see frustration written all over their face. Our coaches know what we are capable of, and they know that if we remain disciplined, committed, and confident in our ability, we'll be able to create scoring opportunities not only for ourselves but also for our team. A good basketball coach knows that if players settle for bad shots, no matter how talented they are, the odds are against the team winning. On the other hand, a team full of talented players with excellent shot selection will rarely lose.

God, the Coach of all coaches, feels the same way. One of my spiritual brothers, Pastor Pierre Johnson, told me that God grieves when we settle. Think about that! When we settle, it breaks God's heart. He knows He's placed a one-of-a-kind talent and potential inside each of us. Much like our hoops coaches, God knows that despite all the gifts He's personally given every one of us, if we don't patiently run His offense, we will take an L. The loss we take, just as in basketball, will affect not only us but also our team, families, and communities.

The verses for this devotional are God's guarantee of victory. He acknowledges our suffering, yet He assures us it will all be worth it if we just stay patient and run His offense. The ball is in our court—we can listen to God and prevail, or we can get impatient and hijack His offense. And just as we have all experienced at least once on the court, we will likely get subbed out of the game and have a reduced role in His offense.

And 1

- ❑ Run God's play, and save the day. Do it your way, and you won't play.

Drop a Dime

- ❑ Identify a teammate who is settling off the court because they are not following God's instructions. Share this devotional with them, and help them trust in God's offense.

KEEP THAT SAME ENERGY

SOUNDTRACK: "OH LORD" – NF

> *My father taught me,*
> *"Take my words to heart. Follow my commands,*
> *and you will live. Get wisdom; develop good judgment.*
> *Don't forget my words or turn away from them."*
> —Prov. 4:4–5 NLT

We have all had moments in sports and in our walk with Christ when our backs were against the wall. These are the moments when we become prayer warriors, begin to live obediently, and make our relationship with God the number-one priority in our lives.

When we establish an active prayer life and allow God to reign over our lives, at some point we will begin to see the fruit of living such a life both on the court and off. When we do, we will begin to reap the benefits of living the way God has called us to. God has a straightforward command something like this: Keep that same energy.

There was a man at a Wendy's drive-through who attempted to place his order, but the person taking his order was extremely rude and disrespectful. When the man drove up to the window, he told that person to "keep that same energy." The exchange went viral, and "keep that same energy" became a go-to phrase.

"Keep that same energy" merely means to stay consistent and not change up. In the case of the rude worker at Wendy's, the man was simply saying that if you're going to disrespect me when I cannot see you, be that same person when I pull up to the window. Be that same person if I tipped you $20, and be that same person when your supervisor is around.

When you got suspended from the team and diligently prayed for God to give you another chance, when you were on the JV team and had no scholarship offers and allowed God to lead you, or when you were attending FCA as a college senior hoping God would open up the door for you to get to the league, God said not to change up when you level up—just keep that same energy.

The verses from Proverbs assure us that if we follow God's commands, we will continue to thrive. They also urge us to never turn away from God's words. God is not telling us to keep the same energy just to flex on us, but He's telling us this to make sure we stay winning. All too often, we settle for less than what God has for us. We work so hard to secure the bag, but God wants more for us. He doesn't want us to just secure the bag; He wants us to sustain the bag once it's secured. He knows our energy for Him must remain the same as it was when our backs were against the wall and we had no choice but to urgently worship and follow Him.

And 1

- ❏ Identify an area in your life that God is telling you to "keep that same energy."
- ❏ Athletically, reflect back to something you urgently prayed to God for and He answered your prayer.
- ❏ Have you kept that same energy? What has been the result of either maintaining or losing that energy?

Drop a Dime

- ❏ Identify a teammate who needs you to be their accountability partner in order to keep that same energy on and off the court. Share this devotional with them, and ask them if you can be each other's accountability partners.

I'M GONNA NEED THAT SAME ENERGY

SOUNDTRACK: "AWESOME REMIX" – CANTON JONES

> *Worry weighs us down; a cheerful word picks us up.*
> —Prov. 12:25 MSG

It's always great to receive congratulatory praise after we break through, but as we reflect on our accolades and accomplishments, it's the encouragement from God and the godly people He placed in our lives that allows us to hang in with hope when we're knocked down. As we ascended from being overlooked, overwhelmed, and underqualified and develop into all-state players, team captains, or professional athletes, I'm sure we can identify a few people who genuinely believed in us even during those times we did not believe in ourselves.

Proverbs 12:25 tells us that a kind word picks us up. How powerful is that? A genuine word of encouragement is literally all you need to keep going when life knocks you down. Please believe that the world of competitive athletics will, indeed, knock you down. My motivation for writing this is to provide you with encouraging messages to support you on your journey in athletics but, more importantly, support you in life. To convince you why you need to invest in your personal relationship with God, I will simply reference this verse. God is the most encouraging friend you will ever have, and His words are uplifting and powerful enough to pick you up in the darkest times.

In the previous devotional, we discussed how we need to have that same energy toward our relationship with God. In this devotional, we'll look at how we need others to keep that same energy during our periods of adversity as they showed us when we were winning. During the good times, it's hard to separate real people from fake. If you allow God, He will use failure as exposure. Failure will expose how much God cares for you and how much the godly people He has placed in your life (the real ones) care about you. Failure will also expose those who front like they have your back, but actually it's fake love disguised really well.

We must be on guard for the fake lovers whose encouragement is situational. These types of people only encourage you after you've succeeded. They will shout you out on Twitter after you are named conference player of the year, but you'll never hear from them when you're riding the end of the bench. That's not encouragement—that's association. Everybody wants to associate with a pro ball player, a McDonald's All-American, and the big man or big woman on campus, but very few want to invest in players when they're learning their game during the process of pursuit. These types of people that we will all encounter must be identified for what they are—pretenders and distractors disguised as encouragers who want to associate with us only to benefit their selfish agendas.

Gucci Mane once tweeted that we must stop feeding the people in our lives who take their plates to go (@gucci1017, January 30, 2018). In other words, when we are at the bottom, we must pay attention to those who disappear only to reappear when we begin to win again. It's crucial that we identify these people so we will not confuse them with the real ones God has placed in our lives. God knows our futures, which means He knows that life on the hardwood as well as life off it is going to knock us down. Because God loves us, He has not only made Himself and His Word available, but He has also placed people in our lives who will always keep that same energy. When we need them, they will provide us with cheerful messages to pick us up.

And 1

- ❑ Moving forward, I challenge all of you to take five minutes before your games and identify one of your real ones who always encourages you. First, meditate with God and thank Him for placing that person in your life, reflecting on specific moments when they held you down. Then, call or text that person and express your gratitude for the role they've played in your life. As you go out on the court and live out your dreams, make sure they know that they are part of your success.

Drop a Dime

- ❑ Acknowledge a teammate who frequently provides genuine encouragement for you.

HE SEES IT IN YOU

SOUNDTRACK: "THE BEST IN ME" — MARVIN SAPP

> *For God has not given us a spirit of fear and timidity,*
> *but of power, love, and self-discipline.*
> —2 Tim. 1:7 NLT

Trick question: Who's the best coach you've ever had? Some can answer that question without even thinking about it, while many others may have to give that question some deep thought. Regardless of how long it took you to come up with your answer, more than likely you answered wrong.

Before we determine our best coach, let's identify the best trait of our favorite coach. That trait is seeing more in us than we could ever see in ourselves and convincing us of what we are capable of.

Young players don't always understand why their coach is so demanding, but as they spend more time in the presence of their coach, they begin to develop faith in them. They begin to trust that the coach has a plan—not of destruction, but of hope. As soon as promising young players reap the benefits of trusting their coach, their frustration becomes replaced with appreciation, and they realize that without their coach's belief, they would have never gone on to do great things.

I had a player explain how playing for the best coach she's ever had impacted her. As she got to know her coach, she gained confidence in herself because of the coach's belief in her. Her coach told her that he coached only gifted players with one-of-a-kind talents. If a player was on his squad, she must have big game and realize her one-of-a-kind talents were vital to his team's success. Her coach also told her, "If I'm with you, it matters not who's against you." She then had a decision to make. Was she going to believe the many doubters and even her own self-doubts or trust in the affirmative, authentic words of her coach?

The player mentioned here is actually you and me. The coach mentioned is the Coach of all coaches—God. So to answer the question posed at the beginning, God is the best coach we will ever play for, and there's no debating it. Second Timothy 1:7 tells us how God did not give us a timid spirit but placed inside us a spirit of power. The best trait of our Coach—God—is seeing more in us than we see in ourselves. Not only does God see more in us, but He actually placed our strengths in us. He wants to draw us closer to Him so we can be convinced of the power He has personally placed in us.

And 1

- ❏ In the past when you felt overwhelmed, inadequate, and intimidated on the court and in life, how did you respond?
- ❏ After reading this devotional, how will you respond moving forward?

Drop a Dime

- ❏ Identify a teammate who has yet to realize the spirit of power that lies within them. Pray that they draw closer to God so God can reveal to them how powerful they are. Pray for God to work through you to reinforce what He says.

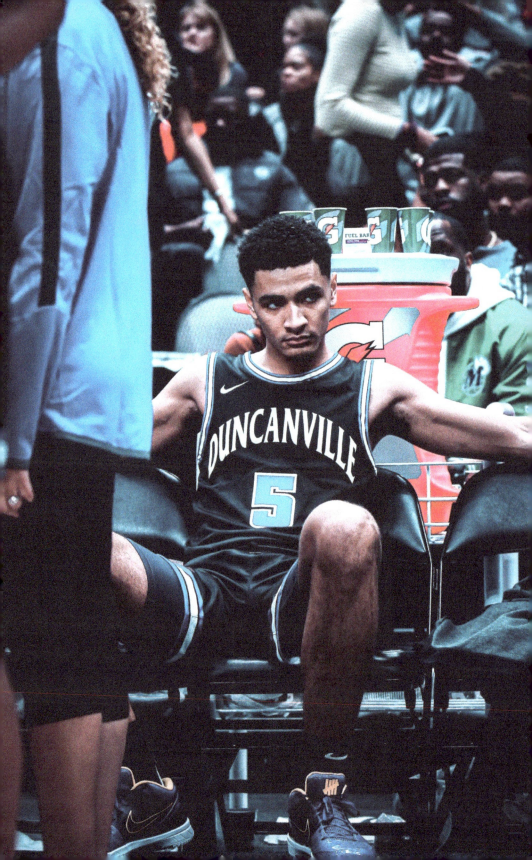

DREAM-CHASING: CATCHING ALL GOD'S GOALS

SOUNDTRACK: "WAY UP (G.O.M. REMIX)" – BIZZLE (FEAT. DATIN, SELAH THE CORNER, BUMPS INF, AND JERED SANDERS)

> *"You didn't choose me, remember; I chose you, and put you in the world to bear fruit, fruit that won't spoil. As fruit bearers, whatever you ask the Father in relation to me, he gives you."*
>
> —John 15:16 MSG

Chances are there is at least one person in your life who needs you to have faith in the dreams God placed in your heart. More than likely, one of those people is someone close to you. Like many others, I used to get disappointed, discouraged, and downtrodden when those closest to me did not believe in my hopes and dreams. There were times when I would not even bother to pursue them because they did not believe in my abilities. Once I got over this hurdle and trusted God despite the doubt from others, I still held resentment toward those close to me who doubted me.

As I continue to mature in my faith, I have come to realize that yes, we all have haters who want to see us fall. But we also have some ride-or-dies in our lives who want to see us make it, but they doubt we're capable of achieving all God has called us to do.

We have to discern between haters and doubters. There's an enormous difference—haters want us to fail, while doubters want us to succeed but lack faith. I used to take it personally when my ride-or-dies did not believe in what I could accomplish. I assumed they did not believe in me. I had to realize their lack of belief in what I could be was a lack of faith in God and not in me. We are all at different places in our faith, and there will be many close to us who cannot support us as we strive to reach God's destiny because they have yet to realize what God is capable of.

I've concluded that God placed some of the people we've resented into our lives and equipped us to reach our dreams in order to make them believers. Not believers in us, but believers in Him.

Maybe you're a role player and your coach doubts you could ever become an all-conference player. But when you become one, God may use that achievement to make your coach a believer in what God can do through you. Maybe your coach doubts you can thrive on the court while pursuing a challenging major, but when you get drafted and graduate with honors, God may use that to develop your coach's faith. Your mom might roll her eyes when you tell her you're going to buy her a house when you go pro. If she does, don't get upset—she loves you but needs you to show her what God can do in your life.

We all have a one-of-a-kind purpose, and today's verse assures us that we are God's number-one draft choice. He chose us to do the amazing long before we chose Him, and as John 15:16 states, God handpicked us to bear fruit. That means when He picked us, He knew we had the potential to be a smashing success in whatever it is He's called us to and prepared us for.

Faith is often a way to prove our love to those close to us. We are all fortunate to have people in our lives who have been a living example of faith for us when we lacked a strong personal relationship with God. As we continue to invest in our relationship with God, we will continually strengthen our faith. This will allow those close to us to witness the fruit that faith produces, which could ignite their faith and forever transform their lives. So keep going, keep grinding, and keep growing.

And 1

- ❏ If there is someone in your life who loves you and wants the best for you—yet they doubt you—let go of the anger. Instead, replace it with a drive to prove God right. Don't say "I told you so," but inspire others to chase their dreams, as well.

Drop a Dime

- ❏ Share this with a teammate who needs to understand the difference between a loving doubter and a hater.

YESTERDAY'S CEILING IS TOMORROW'S FLOOR

SOUNDTRACK: "FOR THE BETTER" – BIZZLE

Don't you see what happens, you simpletons, you idiots?
Carelessness kills; complacency is murder.
—Prov. 1:32 MSG

Once you prove to yourself what you can do on your best day, develop the character to turn your best day into your every day. That's the mindset of a person in relentless pursuit of greatness. I'm incredibly blessed to work with more than a handful of people with this mentality.

Throughout our off-season workouts, Jimmer Fredette, former college basketball player of the year and current professional basketball player, routinely put this notion into practice. During our off-season development program, he'd finish with the Spurs 100, which the San Antonio Spurs frequently use with their perimeter shooters. It calls for a player to shoot 100 NBA 3s off game, like movements and actions.

Jimmer went 81 of 100 his first time doing it. It goes without saying that this was a fantastic feat, especially considering it was at the end of a one-person NBA development workout. To put this into perspective, there are a lot of outstanding players who would be satisfied with shooting 81 of 100 from the free throw line. Jimmer is built differently than most. Many assume he's blessed with incredible talent (and he is), but what separates him is his mindset of greatness. He chases greatness, and once he catches that greatness, he tries to outdo it. As a result, yesterday's greatness becomes today's expectations.

Because of that, he never scored less than 81 in the drill. Once he reached 81, he began to chase 85 and then 90. After a while, he'd reach 82 or 83, and it was as if he was disappointed, I remember when he reached 89, his personal best, he was more upset about the 11 he missed than the 89 he made.

The takeaway of Proverbs 1:32 is this: Complacency is murder on the basketball court as well as in every other area of your life. This verse assures us that the moment we become satisfied with what we did yesterday is the moment our careers, hopes, and dreams begin to die. The way I see it, God did not give us another day to be less than who we were yesterday. In Jesus's name, we ought to stop living in yesterday's success.

During the 2017 season, Jimmer made national news and shocked the world by scoring 73 points in one game. While he was proud of his accomplishment, he was driven to level up. The following season, he scored 75 points, 40 of which were in the fourth quarter. Knowing Jimmer, it's only a matter of time before he goes for 80. Your career high was good enough yesterday, but it ain't good enough today. The character you had yesterday was good enough for who you were, but it ain't good enough for who you can be tomorrow. God has placed His Spirit inside us, and when activated, that Spirit will continue to one-up previous achievements.

And 1

- ❏ Previously, when you accomplished major achievements on the court as well as off the court, how did you respond? Were you satisfied, or did you keep climbing for more in God's name?
- ❏ After reading this devotional, what will your response be moving forward?

Drop a Dime

- ❑ In the future, when one of your teammates achieves success on the court or off, share this devotional with them and challenge them to guard against complacency and to keep grinding for more.

FOLLOW THROUGH WITH FAITH

SOUNDTRACK: "DO IT AGAIN" — ELEVATION COLLECTIVE (FEAT. TRAVIS GREENE AND KIERRA SHEARD)

Faith shows the reality of what we hope for;
it is the evidence of things we cannot see.

. . .

By faith we understand that the entire universe was formed
at God's command, that what we now see did not come from
anything that can be seen.

. . .

And it is impossible to please God without faith. Anyone who
wants to come to him must believe that God exists and that he
rewards those who sincerely seek him.
—Heb. 11:1, 3, 6 NLT

For we were saved in this hope, but hope that is seen is not hope;
for why does one still hope for what he sees?
—Rom. 8:24 NKJV

As those who have a passion for the game of basketball and have had our lives positively impacted by the game, we should be grateful for the faith of James Naismith, the inventor of our game.

Like a good shooter, Naismith's faith had follow-through. As mentioned in the Introduction of this book, Naismith hoped to help young people develop a deeper connection with God and develop Christlike character. His hope fueled his faith, which led him to think outside the box and take a peach basket and a round ball and invent a new sport.

Personally, through the game of basketball, I have developed lifelong friendships, had a college education paid for, and made a living for myself. Had it not been for hoops, I may have never gotten to know God on a personal level. In college, I discovered that the only things I could consistently count on to get me through the highs and lows of basketball were God's love, support, and guidance.

God has also used me to positively impact thousands of young hoopers all over the world. I have traveled to other countries with Athletes in Action to promote Christ, and through my player development program, I have followed Naismith's lead and influenced players, even supporting young NBA star Trae Young in his faith walk.

I don't mention what basketball has done for me and through me to brag but to convict and convince. The same God who led Naismith to take a peach basket and invent a game that has impacted millions of lives for Christ is the same God who's convincing you to do the following:

- Have faith in what God has placed in your heart and not in what you see (Heb. 11:1).
- Please God with your faith (Heb. 11:6).
- Realize that you have to hope in what you cannot see (Rom. 8:24).

I know it's difficult to follow hope and trust through God instead of being led by what you see, but what if Naismith had trusted what he saw and not what he hoped for? If he had, there would be no basketball, and I'm sure your life and my life would be totally different.

Place yourself in his shoes for a moment. Can you imagine God giving you such a dream? What do you think others said to him when he showed up with a peach basket and a round ball claiming God was calling him to invent a new sport? I imagine he was laughed at, talked about, and dismissed—not to mention the number of people who assumed he'd lost his mind.

After hearing how Naismith followed through with his faith, I hope we all dare to do the same, understanding that our faith, or lack thereof, impacts more people than we could ever imagine. During those times of doubt, remember that someone you've never even met, and possibly never will meet, needs you to have hope in God's dreams for your life, just as you and I needed James Naismith to have faith in his dream.

And 1

- ❑ Could you imagine your life without basketball? In your journal, list how your life would be different if basketball were never invented.
- ❑ Where is God calling you to have faith in Him and go for it, like Naismith did?

Drop a Dime

- ❑ Encourage a teammate to hope in what they cannot see, have faith in God, and go for it.

CHANGE THE TEMPERATURE—
DON'T JUST CHECK IT

SOUNDTRACK: "LIGHT SHINE BRIGHT" – TOBYMAC (FEAT. HOLLYN)

Around midnight Paul and Silas were praying and singing hymns to God, and the other prisoners were listening. Suddenly, there was a massive earthquake, and the prison was shaken to its foundations. All the doors immediately flew open, and the chains of every prisoner fell off! The jailer woke up to see the prison doors wide open. He assumed the prisoners had escaped, so he drew his sword to kill himself. But Paul shouted to him, "Stop! Don't kill yourself! We are all here!"

The jailer called for lights and ran to the dungeon and fell down trembling before Paul and Silas. Then he brought them out and asked, "Sirs, what must I do to be saved?"

They replied, "Believe in the Lord Jesus and you will be saved, along with everyone in your household."

—Acts 16:25–31 NLT

But he said to me, "My grace is sufficient for you, for my power is made perfect in weakness." Therefore I will boast all the more gladly about my weaknesses, so that Christ's power may rest on me.

—2 Cor. 12:9 NIV

Do you know the difference between a thermometer and a thermostat? A thermometer can only check the climate, while a thermostat, because of its connection to a higher power, has the power to change the climate. If your team maximizes its potential, it's because there's a thermostat among your squad who adjusts the environment when needed. However, if your team is falling short, more than likely the root of the problem is that your team is full of thermometers who can check the temperature, talk about the temperature, and complain about the temperature, yet no one has stepped up as a thermostat to change things.

In athletics and in other areas of our lives, we would all love to be thermostats and positively change the environment for us and those we care about, but most of us doubt we are capable. Those of us who doubt we're capable of such a change are right—if we attempt to make this change in our own power, we have no chance. We are no different than a thermometer. It's the higher power that the thermostat is connected to that is the source of its ability to change the climate. In the same way, it's not you who's going to change the environment of your team in the midst of a three-game losing streak, and it's not going to be you who changes the vibe of the off-season to go from finishing last to getting an NCAA tournament bid in the upcoming season. It's going to be the Higher Power you are connected to.

In today's verses, Paul is our trailblazer. He explains how being connected to God can allow God to work through us and do what only He can do. While imprisoned, Paul was praying and singing to God, which God used to change the climate. The other prisoners heard Paul and were so moved that they did not escape prison even when given the chance. The jailer, who was about to kill himself because he assumed all the prisoners would escape, was so blown away that no one had left that he immediately gave His life to God.

The verse from 2 Corinthians shows that Paul realized he was at his best when he was at his weakest. Paul knew he had to stay connected to God in order to be a climate-changer for God. If you didn't pay your utility bill, you would not be able to use the thermostat to change the environment because there would be no connection to the source. As hoopers for Christ, we will have no power to supernaturally alter the climate of our team if we do not continue to invest in our relationship with God.

And 1

- ❏ How's the climate of your team? Are there areas in which the climate needs to be adjusted? How can God work through you to change things?

Drop a Dime

- ❏ Share this devotional with some of your teammates, and challenge them to connect to God to be positive climate-changers for the team.

DON'T JUST SECURE THE BAG—SHARE IT

SOUNDTRACK: "BLESS UP" – KORYN HAWTHORNE

> *Eat honey, dear child—it's good for you—and delicacies that melt in your mouth. Likewise knowledge, and wisdom for your soul—Get that and your future's secured, your hope is on solid rock.*
>
> —Prov. 24:13–14 MSG

Don't view the athletic journey God has you on as a vacation destination, or that once you secure your bag, it's time to kick up your feet, indulge, and relax. See it as a business trip. God's not giving you the power to secure your bag just for you—He's empowering you to do His work. He's promoting you because He's entrusted you to influence, inspire, and transform those around you through His power.

Wisdom needs to come with a huge caution sticker that reads, "Caution: know the difference between societal, worldly, trendy wisdom and godly wisdom—often they contradict one another." That is why we must develop a personal relationship with God so others cannot punk us into confusing the two.

This comes into play as we attempt to secure bags. Societal wisdom will lead you to view securing bags as the ultimate goal, while godly wisdom expects us to use our athletic blessings to serve others. We can use godly principles and achieve success, or secure bags, but if we do not have His wisdom, not only will everything we've grinded for eventually crumble but we will not fulfill His purposes. As we commit ourselves to watching film, lifting weights, and doing all the things required for us to win, our thoughts should be consumed with how we will allow God to use us once He's blessed us.

As it relates to your bag, here are some God-led levels:

1. See the bag – We all have God-given dreams, and those dreams drive us to set goals.
2. Chase the bag – Once we set goals and let God lead us, we will develop enough conviction to chase down our dreams.
3. Secure the bag – Our relentless pursuit of our goals produces a daily discipline that provides the habits we need to secure the bag.
4. Sustain the bag – This is where the verses from Proverbs 24:13–14 come into play. Wisdom is what we need as we prepare to sustain our bag. Once we possess His knowledge, which He gives freely to those who seek it, then we will be guaranteed a bright, sustained future.

Many never even think about level 4. When I was in level 1, I never developed the mindset needed to sustain the bag, I never even knew that was a level; I just assumed that once I secured it, that was it. I believed I had made it and that the grind was over—and as a result, the bag I'd worked so hard to secure was gone before I could enjoy it. As I grew closer to God, He revealed another level:

5. Share the bag – Once we secure and sustain the bag, we are now prepared to fulfill God's purpose—share our bag. God created us all to have a bag, and the bag He created us to have is big and one-of-a-kind. God created us to have a big bag to give to those in need of what we have the same way others have something in their bags that we need.

DON'T JUST SECURE THE BAG—SHARE IT

Our bag has to be big enough to help others, and that is why level 4 is so important. Unless you sustain your bag, you can't share your bag and fulfill the purposes God called you to fulfill.

And 1

- ❑ I'm assuming you have visualized and strategized about securing bags. How much time have you given to sustaining and sharing bags once they are secured?
- ❑ What are your motives for securing bags? To indulge in selfish desires? Or to allow God to use your secured bags to support His Kingdom?

Drop a Dime

- ❑ As you and your teammates begin to visualize yourselves securing bags, ensure your teammates are prepared for levels 4 and 5, and share this devotional with them.

REPRESENT

SOUNDTRACK: "NEVER WOULD HAVE MADE IT" – TEYANA TAYLOR

Let every detail in your lives—words, actions, whatever—be done in the name of the Master, Jesus, thanking God the Father every step of the way.
—Col. 3:17 MSG

And whatever you do or say, do it as a representative of the Lord Jesus, giving thanks through him to God the Father.
—Col. 3:17 NLT

Does every detail of what we do on the court represent Jesus? I know that's a tough question to answer. It's tough for me, as well. Here's another tough one: Do we devote time to thinking about how we can honor God with how we play, or do we spend all our time praying God will allow us to play well so we can reach our own selfish goals? If we want to follow God's Word, Colossians 3:17 tells us we must represent Jesus.

If we are going to keep it 100 with all God has done for us athletically, the least we can do is honor Him and express our gratitude with our approach and character on the court. If this verse impacted you as it did me, you are experiencing a deep conviction to look yourself in the mirror and make some immediate changes.

Competitive basketball culture will convince us that we get a pass for using profanity on the court, but if we use Colossians 3:17 as the standard to determine whether we're honoring God, we don't get a pass to drop an F-bomb when the 50–50 block-charge call goes the other way. This verse (as The Message translates it) tells us that every detail of our play, including our words and actions, should be done in a way that represents God. The New Living Translation states that when we step on the court, we are representatives of Jesus. I know the ref will make a horrible call at your expense, and I'm not saying we shouldn't be upset when that happens. I'm just saying that even in the midst of our frustration, we should keep in mind that this game is being covered by the media, some in the stands are capturing it on Snapchat, and, if you are playing at a high enough level, it's being broadcast on national television.

The verse states that in every detail and in whatever we do, we represent Christ, not just during times of convenience. When a fan asks to take a picture with us, when we're on the road and the student section is going in on us, when a coach calls us out in practice, or when we're out to eat at a team dinner, we need to remember Who we represent. Even if you disagree with the ref, even if you have to say no to an interview or an autograph, there is a way to handle those situations while accurately representing Christ. Keep in mind that you can't change what you conform to. Just because this is the current climate of sports culture does not mean we should conform to it. As athletes for Christ, we must ask God to reveal where He wants us to be culture-changers.

It's important to me that I acknowledge I am still a work in progress in this area. As a player, and even now as a trainer, I have been guilty of giving myself a pass for my language and my on-court temperament. As I meditate on this verse in God's presence, I am convicted that He's challenging us to change the culture and to stop giving ourselves and those we influence a pass.

REPRESENT

And 1
- ❏ Look yourself in the mirror, and determine whether you have been giving yourself a pass with your on-court language and temperament.
- ❏ Implement a plan of action to not conform to the culture but to change the culture for God's purposes and through His power.

Drop a Dime
- ❏ Recruit a few teammates to join you in positively changing the culture and not conforming to it.
- ❏ Allow God to lead you and your teammates to establish standards and habits that will accurately represent Him.

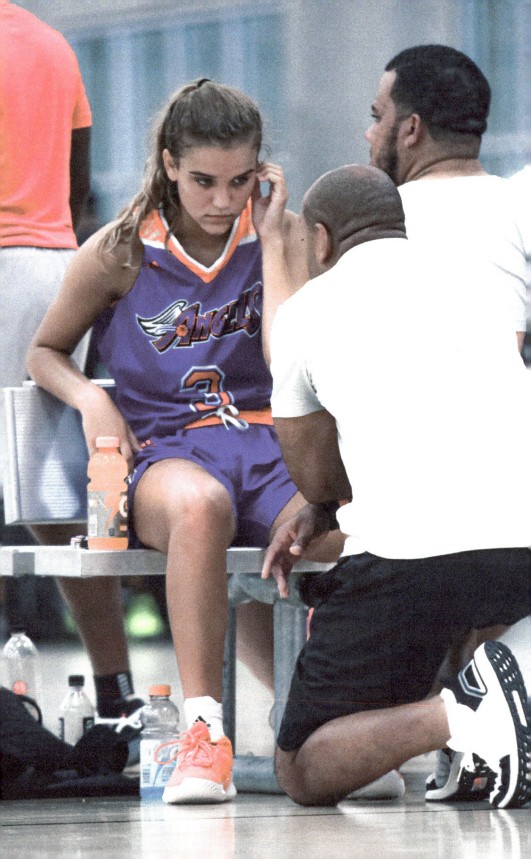

LET GOD BOOK YOUR FLIGHT

SOUNDTRACK: "MY GOD" – J. MONTY

*So let it grow, for when your endurance is fully developed,
you will be perfect and complete, needing nothing.*
—James 1:4 NLT

When God is your travel agent, He'll never book a direct flight to transport you from where you are to where you are going. God's itinerary for your destiny is never going to be the shortest route, nor will it be the cheapest. In fact, more often than not, it will be the longest and most expensive route filled with a number of purposeful layovers.

It's easy to get discouraged when your path seems to take longer and cost more than the paths of others. Don't get frustrated—it's part of God's divine itinerary to strategically transport you from where you are to where He wants to take you.

If we had it our way, we'd approach God's destination for our athletic careers and life like we book flights. When we book a flight, we look for the cheapest and quickest route, but that approach will cost you as you travel toward your athletic and life destinations. God knows that the quickest and cheapest route will get us to our destination, but we will not have acquired the skills, character, integrity, and experiences that are needed to thrive at our destination once we reach it.

His itinerary, which may be turbulent at times, will call for us to make stops at places we'd prefer to fly over. These stops include failure, getting cut, getting benched, being ridiculed by the media, having a coaching change in the middle of our careers, going through a four-game losing streak, being overlooked, being under-resourced, and living outside our comfort zones. While these stops may be uncomfortable at the time, we will leave each stop better prepared for success than we were before we arrived at them.

The ball is in your court. You can choose to book your own flight, select the cheapest and quickest route, and avoid God's layovers. Or you can allow Him to make your travel plans. Your endurance will be fully developed, perfect, and complete, needing nothing, as James 1:4 says. If you do, you will be prepared to thrive once you reach the destination of your dreams, both on the court and in your walk with Christ.

And 1

- ☐ Go back to a time when you made a "direct flight" on your own instead of allowing God to make your travel plans, both athletically and in your journey of life with God. In your journal, list these times, along with the results.
- ☐ Identify an area, both on the court and off, where you need to surrender to God and allow Him to make the itinerary.
- ☐ List those areas, along with why you are reluctant to give those plans to God and a specific plan of action to allow Him to take over.

Drop a Dime

- ☐ Spend time in God's presence, and allow Him to reveal to you a teammate who needs to trust Him and let Him make the travel plans for their life and career. Share this devotional with them and encourage them to apply the "And 1s."

CLOSE WHAT'S DRAINING YOUR BATTERY

SOUNDTRACK: "COME WITH US" – DERAJ (FEAT. NOBIGDYL. & BREEKAY)

> *But I am afraid that as the serpent deceived Eve by his cunning, your thoughts will be led astray from a sincere and pure devotion to Christ.*
>
> —2 Cor. 11:3 ESV

I remember when I got my first iPhone. There was nothing like it. I overindulged on downloading apps—I had an app for everything. Of course, I had my essentials: a Bible app, ESPN, NBA, Bleacher Report, Twitter, Instagram, Facebook (don't judge me—this was years back when Facebook was still cool), and a few others. I also downloaded several apps I did not need and did not use.

After I'd had my phone for a few weeks, I was glad to be part of #teamapple. Everything was great, but the only problem was that my phone was always dying fast. Since I was in business for myself as a basketball trainer, it was vital that my phone was charged up. I attempted to solve this problem on my own, and no matter what I did, I was unsuccessful. I reduced the time I was on the Internet, I avoided recording videos, didn't answer incoming phone calls, and replied back with a text. I even got so desperate that I toggled my phone to airplane mode when I could.

My attempts not only prevented my battery from being drained but also compromised the success of my business. While my iPhone was terrific and had the potential to do everything, it had minimal use because of its drained battery.

I finally went to the Apple Store, and after checking my phone and laughing at me, they merely double-clicked the home button and saw that I had all my apps running in the background. I thought I had a defective phone with minimal value but found out my phone just had too much activity going on. I had no use for 90 percent of the apps that were open—they were just taking up space on my phone and draining my battery. After my visit to the Apple Store, I decided to delete unnecessary apps, make sure I closed apps I wasn't using, and purchase a chargeable battery case. I made sure my battery remained charged so my phone could function at its potential.

As it relates to your basketball career, are you not able to reach your potential on the court because you have too many apps open? Do you have any apps that are just taking up space and need to be deleted? Do you care enough about your basketball career and walk with Christ to take action and close the things in your life that are draining your battery? Will you delete the toxic stuff in your life that should not even be part of your life? Will you take God everywhere you go so He can serve as your chargeable battery case and keep you charged up?

Paul writes to us in 2 Corinthians 11:3 to remember that the same devil who tricked Eve will do the same thing to us if we allow him to. God gives us enough charge to do what He's called us to do on the court and in our lives. If we choose to allow things that He did not anoint us to pursue to drain our spiritual battery, we will fall short of our potential.

God didn't charge us up to:

- Be club gods.
- Build up our body count.
- Live for likes on IG.
- Send nudes on Snap.

He charged us up to:
- Use our gifts to glorify Him and help His people.
- Overcome haters on earth and the devil in hell.
- Be difference-makers and Kingdom-builders through basketball.
- Enjoy the gift of playing the game we love and not take it for granted.

God will give us just enough battery to overcome adversities such as not getting a scholarship offer, going undrafted, and not playing. He will also give us enough battery to sustain being a starter or an All American and leading our team as a captain, but He won't provide us with so much battery that we can burn the candle on both ends. If we use God's power to satisfy agendas that are not according to His purposes, we will eventually lose the ability to hold the charge needed to get W's for Him on and off the court.

And 1

- ❑ Take at least 15 minutes this week to meditate on your "spiritual battery" and allow God to lead you to delete and close what's draining your battery.
- ❑ In your journal, keep a list of what God has revealed to be draining your battery.

Drop a Dime

- ❑ Identify a teammate who has too many apps draining their battery.
- ❑ Approach them about being one another's accountability partner for deleting apps that are preventing both of you from thriving in sports and for Christ.

DON'T GET BIG-HEADED

SOUNDTRACK: "BY CHANCE" — LECRAE & ZAYTOVEN (FEAT. VERSE SIMMONDS)

Because of the extravagance of those revelations, and so I wouldn't get a big head, I was given the gift of a handicap to keep me in constant touch with my limitations. Satan's angel did his best to get me down; what he in fact did was push me to my knees. No danger then of walking around high and mighty! At first I didn't think of it as a gift, and begged God to remove it. Three times I did that, and then he told me,

My grace is enough; it's all you need.
My strength comes into its own in your weakness.

Once I heard that, I was glad to let it happen. I quit focusing on the handicap and began appreciating the gift. It was a case of Christ's strength moving in on my weakness. Now I take limitations in stride, and with good cheer, these limitations that cut me down to size—abuse, accidents, opposition, bad breaks. I just let Christ take over! And so the weaker I get, the stronger I become.
—2 Cor. 12:7–10 MSG

This passage is quite popular, and we as athletes should keep it close at all times. We have all had our big-headed moments in sports when we were immature. As Paul reflects on his maturation, he realizes that his weaknesses prevented him from having a big head. And if he had a big head, he would not have been able to accomplish what God equipped him to do.

When we look at both life and athletics from an immature perspective, we can complain to God about our weaknesses and limitations, only to realize as we mature that our weaknesses were a vital ingredient in His championship recipe for our lives.

If the Apostle Paul were a basketball player, he'd be Derek Fisher, who had a long list of limitations. Fisher did not go to a blue-blood program such as Duke, Kansas, Arizona, or North Carolina. He went to the University of Arkansas Little Rock. He is not uber-athletic and is generously listed at 6'. He does not play above the rim, is not a great finisher, and is not great at creating. When he dribbles, no one is going to mistake him for Kyrie Irving or Jamal Crawford.

But despite his limitations, Fisher played in the league for 17 years and is ranked ninth all-time in career post-season three-pointers made. Most impressively, he is a five-time NBA champion. He is uncommon in his approach to his weaknesses. Much like Paul, Fisher approaches his shortcomings from a mature perspective. It's as if he said to himself, "I am who I am, and I know my limitations. Because I know my limitations, I will be great despite my limitations. I'm smart enough to know I can't do much on my own, but if I do what I'm capable of, I can do great things."

Fisher has never averaged more than 11 points in a season, he's never been on an all-star team, and he's never been on an all-NBA team. However, throughout his career, Fisher was hardworking, humble, and selfless. He put the team first and sacrificed, and he played to his strength of shooting the basketball. Instead of getting discouraged with what he struggled with, he focused on being great at what he does great. He's humble enough to admit that he's not capable of being the star player, and because of that, he is a five-time champion.

So many times in life, we miss out on championship moments because we are not humble enough to accept that we are not good enough to do it alone. We begin to arrogantly think we can reach greatness without God's leadership, and so, out of love, God gives us limitations to prevent us from getting a big head. He wants to develop humility in us like both Paul and Fisher had so we, too, will begin to win championships in life. D Fish may not be a lot of things, but he is a five-time NBA champion. That's more championships than Lebron, D Wade, Melo, Shaq, Karl Malone, KD, and many others.

Embrace your weaknesses, because it's part of God's plan, and never allow others to use your God-placed inadequacies to label you. Others will use labels of weaknesses to limit you, but if you trust God, He will use them to make you a champion.

And 1

- ❑ In your journal, list your gifts of handicaps overall and as an athlete.
- ❑ Take time to rejoice with God for the weaknesses He's given you, knowing that, like Paul, His strength works best in your weaknesses.

Drop a Dime

- ❑ Encourage a teammate to let go of their insecurities. Share this devotional with them so they will understand that their handicaps are a blessing from God.

STRAIGHT FACTS, NO GAS

SOUNDTRACK: "BLESSUP" – JOR'DAN ARMSTRONG

Then Jesus gave the following illustration:
"Can one blind person lead another?
Won't they both fall into a ditch?"
—Luke 6:39 NLT

Faithful are the wounds of a friend [who corrects out of
love and concern], But the kisses of an enemy are deceitful
[because they serve his hidden agenda].
—Prov. 27:6 AMP

Low-grade gasoline will ruin the engine of a luxury car. Luxury car owners understand that only premium gas can fuel their vehicle. There are instructions next to the gas cap of a luxury car that read "premium fuel only." We must realize that God provides us similar instructions about the fuel we take in. We are not common, but as Psalm 139:13–14 explains, we are God-shaped from the inside out, breathtaking and wonderfully made. Because we are premium, we cannot take in bad gas.

In Luke 6:39, God informs us that following a blind person will not keep us on the road to success, but instead, we will be led into the ditches of disaster.

So often on the court and in life, we allow those with no vision, ambition, and drive to gas us up with invalid compliments. If we allow their words to affect us, we won't be able to level up. In the era of social media, low-grade gas can come at us early and often. We must continue to invest in our personal relationship with God to discern which gas, or compliments, we ought to allow to impact us and which ones we need to stay away from.

Affirmation that's based on God's truth will indeed encourage us to continue on the path God has called us to journey, while compliments from the ungodly can blind and distract us from the growth that's needed for what's next. Keep in mind what Cornelius Lindsey said: "If you live off a man's compliments, you'll die from his criticism."[1] As you continue your climb, live by this creed: Straight facts and no gas! All that means is that we are mature enough to embrace the truth, and we know that those who tell us only what we want to hear and not what we need to hear probably have an ungodly agenda, as stated in Proverbs 27:6.

When ungodly people attempt to give you non-premium gas, remain mindful that it takes 13 hours to build a Toyota Corolla and six months to make a Rolls Royce. As people of God, we have to know we will not reach our Rolls Royce stage until we are called home to heaven. Until then, we are a work in progress, and we can't afford to ruin our engine with lousy gas as we're en route to our destination.

And 1

- ❑ Develop a strategy to identify the difference between premium gas and low-grade gas.
- ❑ In your journal or in your notes, list the characteristics of both premium and low-grade gas.

---

1. "Cornelius Lindsey Quotes," *Goodreads*, accessed July 9, 2020, https://www.goodreads.com/author/quotes/6908785.Cornelius_Lindsey.

Drop a Dime

- Put your squad on game. Once you have identified the difference, educate your teammates so they do not ruin their engines.

YOU CAN HAVE IT YOUR WAY

SOUNDTRACK: "CHANGED" — SNOOP DOGG (FEAT. ISSAC CARREE & JAZZE PHA)

Could it be any clearer? Our old way of life was nailed to the cross with Christ, a decisive end to that sin-miserable life—no longer at sin's every beck and call! What we believe is this: If we get included in Christ's sin-conquering death, we also get included in his life-saving resurrection. We know that when Jesus was raised from the dead it was a signal of the end of death-as-the-end. Never again will death have the last word. When Jesus died, he took sin down with him, but alive he brings God down to us. From now on, think of it this way: Sin speaks a dead language that means nothing to you; God speaks your mother tongue, and you hang on every word. You are dead to sin and alive to God. That's what Jesus did.

—Rom. 6:6–11 MSG

Burger King's motto is "Have it your way," and this story illustrates that you, too, can have it your way. Frederick Haynes III of Friendship-West Baptist Church in Dallas says to not let people label you, because when they do, they limit what you can become. That's powerfully illustrated in the story of a young man who, by the age of 15, was arrested 15 times. He was arrested so often that those around him, even loved ones, gave up on him and labeled him a lifetime criminal.

Throughout his first 14 arrests, this young man accepted the label others placed on him. During his 15th arrest, it appeared that he had reached the point of no return when he was placed in solitary confinement after getting into a fight with a rival inmate. But what seemed to be a point of no return in his life turned out to be his launching pad. While confined, the young man was alone with nothing but God's presence and a small window. The influential voices of those who'd mislabeled him based on who he used to be were muted. Instead, those voices were replaced with the voice of God who told him who he was going to be. As a result, the young man made a simple declaration to himself that changed everything: "Who I've been is not who I will be."

Through the window, the only thing the young man could see was a basketball court, so he visualized playing basketball to kill time. Once released, he got a job at Burger King, and his so-called former friends he used to run the streets with visited him at work and tried to convince him to go back to living the fast life. Despite this, he stayed true to his new identity.

He went out for basketball and turned out to be extremely talented—so talented, in fact, that he earned a scholarship to the University of Connecticut. He left after his sophomore year and entered the draft. He wound up having a 14-year NBA career, won an NBA championship, amassed more than $83 million in his career, became a published author, and bought a handful of Burger King franchises. Even with the labels others attempted to put on him, Caron Butler had it his way.

The good news is what our passage from Romans states: "Never again will death have the last word. When Jesus died, he took sin down with him, but alive he brings God down to us." Caron's story is an inspiration to all of us that God is more concerned with where we are going than where we have been. As you begin your journey from the old you to the best version of you, remember that your journey begins with a single step. Don't overwhelm yourself by thinking about the entire journey. Just allow God to lead you as you take one step every day. Remember, the recipe for having it your way isn't complicated—all you need is God and a small window. Through that small window, God will give you a sneak peek at what's in store for you and will ignite your hope and drive your dreams.

And 1

- ❏ I've heard that you should never give someone your pen. When you do, you give them the power to write your story. Every day God gives you is an opportunity to take your pen and write your story. While I have not given other people my pen and allowed them to write my story, I have let my past-me write the story of what I could be. As a result, my past once defined me and placed a low ceiling on what I could become in the future.
- ❏ There's power in your pen. Take control of it, and allow God to lead you to write your story. After praying to and meditating with God, start writing your new story in your journal or in your notes.

Drop a Dime

- ❏ Find a teammate who has allowed others to label them by their past failures, and share this story with them. Encourage them to keep dreaming, knowing that it matters not who they have been or what they have done. All God cares about is who they are becoming.

USE YOUR T.O.S

SOUNDTRACK: "FIGHT FOR ME" — GAWVI (FEAT. LECRAE)

Then Jesus said, "Come to me, all of you who are weary and carry heavy burdens, and I will give you rest."
—Matt. 11:28 NLT

He gives power to the weak and strength to the powerless.
—Isa. 40:29 NLT

God is our refuge and strength, always ready to help in times of trouble.
—Ps. 46:1 NLT

I have told you all this so that you may have peace in me. Here on earth you will have many trials and sorrows. But take heart, because I have overcome the world.
—John 16:33 NLT

During my time on staff at Iowa State, we were fortunate enough to have one of the best home courts in college basketball. We played in front of 14,356 every night at Hilton Coliseum. When opposing coaches came to compete in front of the Hilton Magic, they were not afraid to use their time-outs early and often. They knew that the hostile environment could cause their team to not perform at their optimal level.

The thing about playing on the road, especially in tough environments, is that it's not comfortable. As a result, it can cause teams to get distracted, feel anxious, lose confidence, panic when the opponent makes a run, and—if they are not gritty enough—even wave the white flag and give up.

Great coaches know the pulse of their teams, so they know when to call a time-out and what to say during the time-out. Maybe they need to call a special play to get the team going or switch defenses to take the crowd of the game. Maybe they need to allow their tired team to catch their breath or instill confidence in them and remind them how special they are. Whatever the time-out calls for, good coaches know what buttons to push and when to push them.

At the conclusion of a time-out huddle, a good coach always tells their players how many time-outs are remaining. They also remind players that if things aren't going their way, they can always call a time-out. God does the same for us as we navigate through the day.

In today's sports culture, it can be quite challenging for a coach or a player to compete at a high level while pleasing God. It's so challenging that I don't believe we can do it without using multiple time-outs daily. As Christians, our mindsets here on earth should be no different than the opponents I faced at Iowa State. They knew that because they were in a hostile environment, they'd have to call more time-outs than they otherwise would, and they understood that winning in hostile environments would be impossible without time-outs. The good news for us is that God has provided an unlimited supply of time-outs. The verses associated with this devotional are just a few of the many verses we can use during our daily time-outs with God. They ensure us that God will focus us when we get distracted, calm us down when we are upset, speak greatness into us when we are overwhelmed, and assure us that His plan will prevail when it appears we are doomed.

And 1

- ❏ Devote some of your quiet time with God over the next few days to identifying time-out verses of your own. Then write them down in your journal.
- ❏ Refer to them as frequently as possible when the enemy is making a run at you. Remember, God's rules are different, and we can use as many time-outs as possible.
- ❏ DM me on Twitter or Instagram @GODxbasketball with a high-quality image of you playing. Send me some of your go-to time-out verses, quotes, and phrases. I will create a time-out card we can use to encourage others to take time-outs daily.

Drop a Dime

- ❏ Send a time-out card to a teammate every day for the next seven days.

GOD'S VISION > THE BIG PICTURE

SOUNDTRACK: "SET ME FREE" – LECRAE, YK OSIRIS

*Jesus said, "If? There are no 'ifs' among believers.
Anything can happen."*

*No sooner were the words out of his mouth than the father cried,
"Then I believe. Help me with my doubts!"*

—Mark 9:23–24 MSG

As you continue to get to know God more personally, you'll realize that you cannot out-dream God. The God-placed visions inside you are so much bigger than your big picture. While that may seem like a good thing, it can be unsettling as well.

The dreams that God places in our minds and hearts are colossal. They are so big that they may not make sense, and that feeling of uncertainty can lead to becoming unsettled. For myself, I would have a conviction in my soul that I was created to do the unimaginable, but then I would look at myself in the mirror and see all my flaws and inadequacies. I'd start to believe that either my mind was playing tricks on me or that God had made a mistake and given these big dreams to the wrong person.

I'd think to myself that there was no way I could do what I felt God was calling me to do. I told myself that I can't write a book because I struggled in English class. I said I can't train high-level players since my college career was trash. I knew I couldn't start my own business because I majored in sociology. Because of my incorrect thoughts, I could not rely on myself to believe I was capable of fulfilling the visions for my future. Instead, I relied on others. That did not go so well, either—I was hoping people would believe in me and my big dreams when I doubted, but that wasn't the case.

It has taken me a while, but I have finally figured it out. Your God-placed dreams will not activate without God-led faith. For the longest time, I was hustling backward, relying on myself to push me toward my gigantic dreams. That was a big fail. I then looked to others, and that was another fail. Finally, I allowed God to take over my life completely. When He did, my unbelief was healed, and I began to take steps toward living in a way that was so much bigger than the big picture. Along the way, God revealed to me that His visions for my life are far too big for me to handle and that when I attempt to strive toward them in my own power, I have no chance.

God has perfect credit, and when He finances a vision inside you, He does not need a cosigner. Along with the dreams God has placed in us through His Holy Spirit—you know, the intimidating ones that make no sense—He's also provided us with enough to fulfill them. You don't need to go out and get those close to you to sign off on them; instead, you need to draw closer to Him and ask Him to heal your doubts and unbelief. When you do, your faith in Him will be activated and your unbelief healed. God will do what only He can do through you.

As you commit to pushing past your big picture and pursuing the God-placed and God-sized dreams that lie within you, hold onto this power thought: *Through God's power, for God's purposes.*

Never forget that it's only through God's power that you will reach your dreams, and it's for His purposes that He gave you the vision in the first place.

And 1
- ❏ Reflect on a time when God's plan for you was bigger than your big picture.
- ❏ Have you ever lost confidence as you attempted to pursue God's vision for your life because you relied on your own strength or were looking for someone else to cosign? If so, list those times in your journal, along with the results.

Drop a Dime:
- ❏ As we invest in a personal relationship with God, we will develop a courage and conviction to go after God's plans for our lives. Do your part to encourage a teammate to invest in Christ so they, too, can live the life God called them to live.

BUILD THE FOUNDATION

SOUNDTRACK: "I'LL FIND YOU" – LECRAE (FEAT. TORI KELLY)

God does both the making and saving.
He creates each of us by Christ Jesus to join him in
the work he does, the good work he has gotten ready
for us to do, work we had better be doing.

—Eph. 2:10 MSG

When doors slam shut, haters hate, and it seems everyone else is living their best life while you feel broken down to the point of no return, know this: You are in the best place you could possibly be. While it may appear you've failed and are doomed for despair, maybe, just maybe, God has allowed temporary setbacks and destruction to occur in your life to get you down to the ground. Being on the ground places you in a perfect position to get on your knees and join Him in building a strong foundation for the next stage of your career and life overall. As you read the Bible, you will be frequently reminded of God's plans for your future. And by building a strong foundation, you can sustain success when God leads you to level up and those big plans come to pass.

As athletes, we all have seasons of failure. If we are not careful, we will be so blinded by them that we will mistake God's plan for our future with a knockout punch designed to take us out. When you feel like that, ask yourself if it is possible to build a penthouse minus a strong foundation. I don't think so. To experience the penthouse moments of life, you have to construct a strong foundation down at the bottom. If life has broken you down to the ground, don't complain and feel sorry for yourself. Just take advantage of being down there, and lay the foundation for future success in Jesus's name.

I tell athletes all the time that if basketball has never broken them down to tears, they must not love it. If you have never had valleys so long, deep, and dark that you don't know if and how you are going to recover, you are not going hard enough. When these uninvited yet unavoidable dark moments present themselves, I want you to hold onto the following truths about the ups and downs of your journey:

> People laughed, counted me out, and were even disappointed when they saw me on the ground. They assumed I failed—Nah, I ain't fail. God called me down to build me up and allow Him to level me up. He said the foundation I currently have is good for where I was, but it's nowhere near strong enough for where He's taking me. He invited me to join Him in building a strong foundation to support my future success. But y'all go ahead and keep laughing, and don't mind us. We'll be down here building a foundation strong enough to support and sustain a penthouse. And when we are all done, I will honor God's command and make sure the penthouse is used to serve His purposes and His people, even those who once laughed at me, hated on me, and were disgusted and disappointed with me when they mistook my being on my knees for a result of self-inflicted failure.

And 1

- ❑ Identify at least one time on the court and one off the court when God arranged for you to come down and join Him in building a stronger foundation.
- ❑ Identify an area both on the court and off where you are currently on the ground building a foundation for what's next or where you need to be building a foundation.
- ❑ Have you forgiven those who hated on you, laughed at you, and looked down on you when you were on the ground?
- ❑ If you have not, keep in mind how many times God has forgiven you. Remember that as ambassadors for Christ, we should give the grace and mercy to others that's been provided to us. If you are not ready to forgive, give that hurt to God, and allow Him to change your heart.

Drop a Dime

- ❑ Encourage a teammate who's on the ground building their foundation, and share this devotional with them.

DON'T BE A PAINT-JOB GUY

SOUNDTRACK: "DEEP END" – LECRAE

> *I'll pour pure water over you and scrub you clean.*
> *I'll give you a new heart, put a new spirit in you.*
> *I'll remove the stone heart from your body and replace it*
> *with a heart that's God-willed, not self-willed.*
> *I'll put my Spirit in you and make it possible for you*
> *to do what I tell you and live by my commands.*
> —Ezek. 36:26–28 MSG

When God changes us, He could care less about what we look like externally. He doesn't do cosmetics. He goes to work on us internally by changing our souls and developing our character. When we allow God to transform us internally and establish the character we need to not compromise, we develop a sense of self and, more specifically, a sense of God within ourselves. When that sense of God in ourselves is developed, it gives us the godly instincts to do the godly thing even in the most ungodly situation.

We have all seen or heard about failures due to a lack of spiritual guidance from religious leaders, basketball coaches, successful athletes, and people we look up to in our communities. Before we point a finger and call out the hypocrisy of others during such failures, we should humble ourselves and realize two things. First, we should have compassion for them and pray for them, thanking God for His grace and mercy for them in their situation. We should then realize we are capable of the same type of failures if we do not allow God to transform us internally.

It's worth repeating that my hope for this book is that you are convicted to invest more in your personal relationship with God. He will then organically transform you and produce the instincts to make Christlike character decisions athletically and in every other area of your life. One of my spiritual mentors, Frederick Haynes III, explained it like this: If you had a luxury car with a lousy paint job and a failing engine and could only afford to address one of those issues, which would it be? Unfortunately, many people are paint-job guys—they place a premium on cosmetics over substance. As a result, they look good but lack what's needed internally to go far.

Since we are basketball people, I'll put it like this: If your jump shot was broke and your gear was outdated, but you only had enough money to pay for a shooting coach or to purchase new drip, which would you buy? If you pay for the shooting coach, your shot will improve, but others may make fun of you because your gear is weak. On the other hand, if you invest in the drip, you will look good on the bench but not be able to fulfill your potential as a basketball player because you chose not to invest in the person who was equipped to lead you to maximize your potential.

While basketball is important to all of us, there is a more concerning issue at hand. There is a question we must answer as we look at ourselves in the mirror. Are we going to invest and trust in God and allow Him (as it states in Ezekiel) to change us, replace our engine, and fix our spiritual shot? Or are we going to continue to invest in cosmetics and navigate through life with a pretty paint job and some fresh kicks and yet fall short of living the life and being the player God has called us to be?

And 1

- ❑ Look back and learn from previous mistakes by identifying a time when you chose the paint job over the engine—in basketball and in your journey with Christ. What were the results?
- ❑ List a current situation in which you need to invest in your engine and not your paint job.

Drop a Dime

- ❑ Identify a teammate to keep you accountable to invest in what matters most on the court and off the court, and do the same for them.

HIT THE RESET BUTTON

SOUNDTRACK: "I AM A WINNER" – JEKALYN CARR

> *Since we've compiled this long and sorry record as sinners (both us and them) and proved that we are utterly incapable of living the glorious lives God wills for us, God did it for us. Out of sheer generosity he put us in right standing with himself. A pure gift. He got us out of the mess we're in and restored us to where he always wanted us to be. And he did it by means of Jesus Christ.*
>
> —Rom. 3:23–24 MSG

It might be a blessing in disguise that EA sports discontinued the NCAA College Football video game, because I was addicted. Had it not been discontinued, I'd probably be playing it right now instead of writing this book. I liked to play in Dynasty mode; I strived to string together national titles like Nick Saban at Alabama. To have a shot to win the national title, chances are I'd have to run the table during the regular season and go undefeated. I'm ashamed to admit it, but there were times when I'd lose a game and reset the Xbox before the game would save. After resetting the game, I was able to play the game over and continue to pursue my goal of winning a championship without any penalty. I'd go on to win national titles. My record appeared spotless and allowed me to move on as if the loss never occurred. It mattered not why I lost—I always played knowing that if I took an L, I could just hit the reset button.

Because of this luxury, I played aggressively, confidently, and without the pressure to be perfect. I'm so blessed that through Jesus's blood, I can live life the same way I played NCAA Football. God knew a long time ago that I was not capable of going undefeated, so He sent His perfect and flawless Son to die for me. Not only did He send Him to die for me, but He also sent Jesus to hit the reset button for me so I could live in attack mode as I navigate through life.

There are many times in my walk with God that I struggle to let go of the guilt of my sins. When I feel like I deserve a second chance, I allow myself to receive God's grace. On the other hand, I struggle to take advantage of Jesus hitting the reset button for me when I know I don't deserve it. I hold onto the guilt of my mistakes. I need to receive God's grace and mercy the way I accept resetting my video games. When I hit reset, I forget all about the previous loss and continue pursuing my goals, minus the burden of past failures.

Jesus's death for our sins wiped the slate clean. No matter what happened yesterday, God hit the reset button for us to begin again without any penalty of our previous failures.

I hope this book has served its purpose for you as you navigate through sports and life. I hope you have gotten to know Jesus on a more personal level. I hope that through the basketball analogies, you've become better connected to God's Word. But the ultimate purpose is for you to accept Jesus's gift by accepting Him as your Lord and Savior. If you have not received Him, I pray that you have heard God speaking to you through this book and specifically this devotional.

If you have not accepted Jesus and are ready, say this prayer:

> Lord, I am ready to live for You and through You. I receive You, Jesus, as my Lord and Savior. I thank You for dying a painful death for my sins, and I thank You for rising from

death for me. Your dying for my sins means I am clean, and through You, I am always forgiven, even when I don't deserve it. Because of you, I can always hit the reset button. Because you rose from death, I will never lose hope because the same blood that was in You when you rose is in me. Amen.

And 1

- ❏ If you have already given your life to Christ, take a few moments to commemorate that and remind yourself that you can aggressively live life knowing that when you fall, Jesus hits the reset button.
- ❏ If you have doubts about completely giving your life to God, it's okay. God accepts you right where you are, doubt and all. If you doubt this truth, just open your heart and give God a tryout. Psalm 34:8 tells us to "taste and see that the Lord is good" (NIV). God knows that once you give Him a chance, you'll want Him on your team permanently.
- ❏ If you are a new believer, remember to develop your God Squad—that's a major key for all believers, but new believers especially.
- ❏ I encourage all of you—newcomers to Christ and experienced vets—to add us to your squad by frequently visiting our blog at GODxbasketball.com and giving us a follow on social media @GODxbasketball and me specifically @cultoreordie.
- ❏ We would love for you to share with us your on-court and off-court breakthroughs, along with your on-court and off-court struggles. We want to celebrate your successes. And we not only want to support you through your valleys but also help others through theirs. More than likely, there's someone else going through or about to go through what you are going through.

Drop a Dime

- ❏ Talking to others about their faith can be intimidating, uncomfortable, and awkward. If you are anything like me, as you grow closer to God, you frequently find yourself in an unsettling place where you want to help those close to you grow closer

to God, but you don't know how to or whether you should approach them.
- ❏ For me, just like James Naismith, basketball has often served as an icebreaker that eventually allowed me to be comfortable and organically discuss faith.
- ❏ Maybe this book could be your icebreaker. If so, drop the ultimate dime, and invest in the future of a friend or teammate and gift them a copy of this book.
- ❏ Write a heartfelt note in the inside cover, explaining how this book has impacted you and why you think it will do the same for them.
- ❏ If you feel moved to, share your dime drop with us. Snap a pic of you, the book, and the teammate you purchased it for. Share on social media, and tag us @GODxBasketball with the hashtags #Godxbasketball #droppedthedime.

OVERTIME

YOU'RE DROPPING DIMES FOR GOD, AND YOU AIN'T EVEN KNOW IT

As you continue to transform into the best version of yourself, don't discredit your influence over others.

Even though it feels as though your influence on others is nonexistent, that's not the case, despite the fact that you feel inadequate and unworthy to be God's dime-dropper. Someone is watching you right now, and you are dropping a dime for God by inspiring them to get to know God for themselves.

I was an assistant coach at Missouri Baptist University in 2008. It was by far one of the toughest years of my life. My girl had just dumped me, three people close to me had died, I had no money and no friends, and work was extremely challenging. I assumed my impact on others was minimal at best.

Late in the season, Justin Madden, a freshman walk-on, approached me and asked, "What does it mean to be saved?"

He went on to say that he noticed that my life sucked because of the reasons mentioned above but that despite my adversity, I had a glow about me. He said he'd frequently seen me reading the Bible, listening to my Christian gospel playlist, and having Bible studies at the local coffee shop.

He was blown away that someone whose life appeared to suck could have such a joyous glow. He correctly concluded that my glow came from my faith in God. He told me that he wanted that same glow and gave his life to Christ that day.

Justin is currently a youth pastor and has influenced thousands of youth to give their lives to God.

You need to know that there's a Justin Madden in your life watching you, and they see and want your radiant godly glow. So for their sake and the sake of those they will go on to influence for Christ, keep glowing, and keep growing.

CULTURE CONTRACT

Through God's power, we will not rest until we squeeze every ounce of potential and opportunity out of our talent.

Through this commitment, our talent will take us to heights we never knew existed.

Most importantly, we will never allow our talent to surpass our character.

Through our commitment to our character, we will shine bright like God created us to do and change the world in His name and for His purposes.

Our combination of character and talent will allow others to see God through us without even saying a word.

This isn't my culture, nor is it yours. It's God's, and we are just embracing our small but significant roles.

Promote His culture.

Ignite His culture.

Live His culture.

Do it for His culture.

God x basketball.

Signature: _____ Date: _____

Signature, Accountability Partner: _____ Date: _____

Share it! Encourage others to sign the contract by posting yours on Twitter or Instagram. Be sure to tag us on your post @GODxbasketball #Godsgame #GODxbasketball #culturecontract.

KEEP GOING

I know it's tough right now.

I know it seems as if there's no light at the end of the tunnel.

I know it seems you may as well do wrong because it appears there's no reward for doing right.

I know you feel invisible and your good deeds seem to go unnoticed, while those who take shortcuts and compromise their character seem to win.

I know you feel lonely, misunderstood, and isolated.

I know you're second-guessing yourself and feel you made the wrong decision.

I know everybody's telling you to settle, and everything in you is telling you the same.

I know it seems like you should quit, but I can't let you do that. God is speaking through me to strengthen you.

God told me to tell you to fight just a little bit longer.

God told me that He will never put more on you than you can bear.

God told me that the answer to your "Why me?" question is that you are His warrior. You will never know what you can do through His power if you don't overcome what you are about to overcome.

God told me that when He looks at you, He sees what He created—a diamond. He is just allowing the fires you are going through to transform you from the dusty piece of coal you are now into the bright, shiny, one-of-a-kind diamond you will be. He told me He loves you far too much to allow you to remain a piece of coal.

God told me you'd ask this: "Why can't I just be a diamond right now?"

God told me to tell you that He wants others to see your transformation—those who believe in Him and in you, those who lack faith and need proof, and the haters who laughed and said you would never amount to anything.

God told me that the hell you will overcome to be a diamond will allow you to receive His blessings humbly and, as a result, be a blessing and inspiration to others.

God told me to tell you that no matter what you are going through, His grace is all you need, and His power works best in your weakness.

God told me to tell you that it will all be worth it in the end, and when you get through what you are going through, He will smile and tell you, "Great job, my good and faithful servant."

SOMEONE NEEDS YOU TODAY

There are people in my life today who need me to serve them.

There are people in my life today who need me to forgive them.

There are people in my life today who need me to love them.

There are people in my life today who need me to love myself. (I can't give something I don't possess; I can't love others if I do not love myself.)

There are people in my life today who need me to be happy. (I can't help someone else be happy if I'm not happy.)

There are people in my life today who need me to forgive myself.

There's someone in my life today who needs to grow closer to God. Maybe God will speak through me, and if so, Lord, please prepare and use me. If God doesn't need to use me, I will just pray, and even though I do not know who it is, I rejoice that they are accepting God as the authority in their life.

There's someone in my life today who God needs me to speak to.

There's someone in my life today who is watching me, and as they do, I pray I am hidden and God is visible.

There's someone in my life today who needs me to listen to them.

There's someone in my life today who needs me to see them—see them grow, see them hurting, see them laugh, see them fall, see them overcome. Lord, open my eyes to see what I need to see for You.

There's someone in my life today who needs me to smile.

There's someone in my life today who needs me to use basketball as a vehicle to lead them toward God.

There's someone in my life today who needs me to face my fears.

There's someone in my life today who needs me to be a better person today than I was yesterday.

There's someone in my life today who needs me to chase down my gigantic basketball dreams.

GAME-DAY CHALLENGE

God x Basketball Game-Day Challenge

Taking time to celebrate what God has already done will provide you with faith and expectancy in your future pursuits.

Each game day, take at least 15 minutes in the presence of God and do two things:

1. Reflect on all God's blessings thus far.

   Think about:
   - the doors God opened to allow you to play this game
   - the doors He closed to allow you to play this game
   - the tears cried and the adversity overcome

   Go back to a time when you were younger and playing this game was just a prayer, a distant dream you didn't even know was going to come true.

   Go back to a moment when the obstacle that lay between you and your dream appeared so big that you did not believe you could overcome it. Yet here you are, living out your dream.

   As you do this, simply thank God for all He has done, and share this moment with Him.

2. Identify one person God used to help you be able to play in today's game and live out your dreams.

   a. Once you identify that person, pray to God, thanking Him for that person and their contribution.

b. Pray for that person and their family.
c. Ask God never to allow you to forget their contribution.
d. In God's presence, reflect on what that person did specifically. Determine how you can honor their contribution by how you compete on the court and the character you conduct yourself with off the court.
e. Text that person, and thank them for what they've done for you. Let them know how appreciative you are for their contribution to your success.

The same God who heard and answered that prayer is the same God who will transport you from where you are now to where you are praying to go on the court and in every other area of your life. By taking time to celebrate what God has already done, you will learn faith and expectancy in your future pursuits.

ACKNOWLEDGMENTS

Most importantly, I thank God for deeming me worthy enough to write this book. God, You know I've struggled with validation and worth issues my whole life, and the fact that You chose me to write this book is all the validation I need.

Thank you to the talented photographers who provided images for this book: Kevin Keyser (Keyser Images in Denver, Colorado), Luke Lu (KL6 Photo in Iowa), and my talented sister, Brittany Graham (better known as ItsByBritt, Dallas, Texas). Your images are the ultimate "dime drop."

Thank you to those who supported me financially, donated gym time, and put me up while I traveled the country to raise money during the process of writing and publishing this book. Thank you, Alan B, Rod, Coach P, Bill B, Cody, Jere, G3, Mel, and my parents.

Thank you to those who prayed, affirmed, and encouraged me during moments of doubt, along with those who took time to read and provide feedback through the process. Thank you, Eric V, Sara W, Dr. B, Jere, Q, CJ, Mandi, Sammy, Rod, Mama Nixon, and Mama Byrne.

Thank you to my li'l sisters from the 2018 Iowa State women's basketball team. You, young women, were the ones who inspired me, empowered me, and demanded that I write this book. Thank you, Lex, Adrianna, Nia, Meredith, and Madison.

Thank you, Eric Valerio, for being you and riding for me when I was hard to ride for.

Q and CJ, I'm so thankful for you. You are two of the realest dudes I know in basketball. Thank you for making me a better man.

Blake Ebel, thank you for being my trailblazer.

TC, thank you for being the brother I never had, always believing in me and allowing your mom, Aunt Carolyn, to be my second mom. I know she's so proud of the man you have developed into and the amazing father you have become.

A N' A, I love you all. We will forever be family. No matter where life takes me, I'll rep you all until the death of me. Rest in heaven, Mac Forrest and R.J. Demps. Your legacies will not only be with me for the rest of my life but will live through me, as well.

Thank you to the late Hall of Fame Coach Eddie Sutton and Oklahoma State Basketball for taking me in as your little brother. You all taught me everything I know about basketball.

Chris Dempsey, I will forever be grateful to you for writing the Foreword. There's no better person to write it. Very few know the grind you went through to get where you are today.

Thank you to Steve Prohm and the Iowa State men's basketball program for allowing me to be part of such a special program. I will forever cherish the season I spent as an Iowa State Cyclone.

Lucid Books, thank you! You will never know how much it means to me that your entire team believed in this book and empowered me to be a published author.

Pastor Frederick Haynes III of Friendship-West Baptist Church, Dallas, Texas, without you as my pastor, my life would be totally different. Without you, I would have downsized my dreams a long time ago.

Chauncey Billups, thank you for seeing greatness in me and investing your time in developing my talent as a teacher of the game we both love and as a leader. You are an example by your actions and not just your words.

Mom and Dad, there aren't enough words to express my thanks, but what's understood needs not be explained. Thank you both for holding me down and instilling in me the passion, work ethic, and commitment needed to write this book. Most importantly, thank you for introducing me to my Best Friend, my Rock, and my Savior, Jesus Christ.

Go COUGS and Pioneer Pride!
Stillwater High Class of '99
Washington State Class of '03

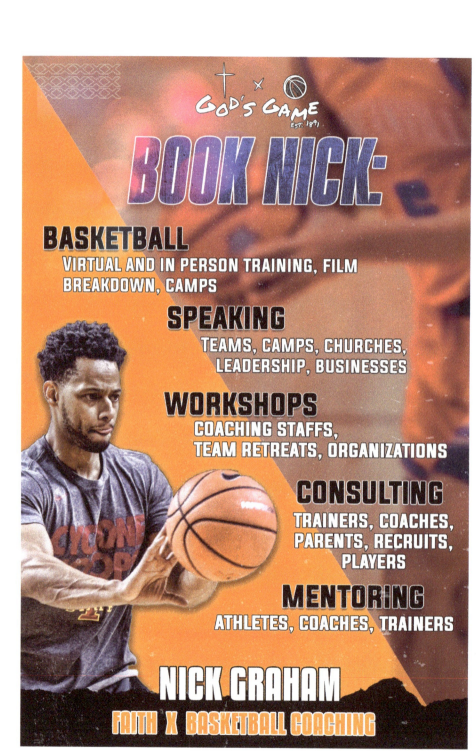

HOLISTIC TRAINING

GOD'S GAME
EST. 1891

Skill Devlopment
IQ Film Breakdowns

✚ ✚ ✚

Character Development
Leadership
Communication

NICK GRAHAM
FAITH X BASKETBALL COACHING

CPSIA information can be obtained
at www.ICGtesting.com
Printed in the USA
LVHW070948130323
741503LV00020B/183